KILL THE CHAMELEON

How business owners can avoid burnout and thrive with clarity and authenticity

MATT LINNERT

KILL THE CHAMELEON

ACKNOWLEDGEMENT

This book wouldn't exist without the unshakable support of my wife, Debbie.

Writing it was a questionable financial and commercial decision. Yet it felt like the right thing to do, something I simply had to do. Debbie didn't flinch. She said, "Go for it."

Our family's support runs deep. My two children, Max and Amelia, encouraged me to believe in myself whenever doubt crept in. They checked in regularly on how the book was progressing, and offered both practical and emotional support whenever I needed it.

Then there's the long list of generous people who helped with early manuscript reading, editing, cover concepts and interior design. This book is the result of a truly collaborative effort, and I'm grateful for everyone who played a part.

To those who said, "I'd love to have a read," your simple words kept the encouragement flowing. It's amazing how a thoughtful gesture can keep momentum alive.

And then we have the heroes of this book. All the people I've had the privilege of walking alongside, bumping into, disappointing, pleasing, annoying and loving.

I'm deeply grateful for everyone who's crossed my path. Each encounter, every shared moment. You've put the life into these words, and without you, this book would not exist.

I've done my best to gather the gold from our experiences, and I hope these pages carry some of that gold back to you.

Every garden has its share of beauty and challenge. Some plants thrive in the environment's soil and sunlight, blossoming with little effort once their roots take hold. Others struggle, straining in conditions they were not built for.

Among the plants there's a chameleon. At first glance, it looks clever – changing its colours to match its surroundings, blending in wherever it lands. But even in the garden, a chameleon isn't truly at ease anywhere. It survives by constant adjustment, never showing its true colours, always shifting to fit what's around it.

Many business owners end up living like that chameleon. They bend themselves to every demand, every expectation, every 'rule' of how success is supposed to look. They keep changing and adapting until they've lost sight of what's right for them, and who they really are. Like the chameleon, they survive – but they don't thrive.

This book is about choosing a different path. About planting yourself in the right soil, tending your business like a healthy garden, and creating success that's rooted in what will work for you according to your nature. To do that, you'll have to kill the chameleon – the part of you that keeps shape-shifting for everyone else – and instead grow a business, and life, that's deeply aligned with your nature.

Killing the chameleon is the doorway to clarity and thriving. It empowers authentic growth and creates a burnout-proof version of you.

First published in 2025 by Matt Linnert

© Matt Linnert 2025
The moral rights of the author have been asserted

All rights reserved. Except as permitted under the *Australian Copyright Act 1968* (for example, a fair dealing for the purposes of study, research, criticism or review), no part of this book may be reproduced, stored in a retrieval system, communicated or transmitted in any form or by any means without prior written permission. No part of this book may be used or reproduced in any manner for the purpose of training artificial intelligence technologies or systems.

All inquiries should be made to the author.

A catalogue entry for this book is available from the National Library of Australia.

ISBN: 978-1-923630-04-8

Book production and text design by Publish Central
Cover design by Julia Kuris, Melissa Horvat and Lexie Wadsworth

Disclaimer

The material in this publication is of the nature of general comment only, and does not represent professional advice. It is not intended to provide specific guidance for particular circumstances and it should not be relied on as the basis for any decision to take action or not take action on any matter which it covers. Readers should obtain professional advice where appropriate, before making any such decision. To the maximum extent permitted by law, the author and publisher disclaim all respon-sibility and liability to any person, arising directly or indirectly from any person taking or not taking action based on the information in this publication.

CONTENTS

Preface | Burnout: the unwanted badge of honour   **xiii**

Burnout and stress for small business owners   xiii
Why this book exists   xiv
How to use this book   xvii

Introduction | When success stops feeling good   **1**

The downward spiral   1
Kill the chameleon   5
What I learnt and how it helps   7

01 | A new platform: attitude towards oneself   **9**

Compassion first   10
You can't please everyone   13
Be yourself   15
Control your tempo   17
One hand in, one hand out   19
Work/life balance – an inside job   22
Meditation to mediation   25
It's a game of perspective   28
Fear of missing out   30
Money can buy happiness   34
Chapter summary   37
Reflective questions for a new platform:
   attitude towards oneself   40

02 | Clarification: what's right for you   47

Define success your way	50
Natural inclinations	52
Getting in the flow	56
What drains your energy?	59
Observing reactivity and triggers	63
Rebalancing your energy	66
Clarification tools and tips	69
Chapter summary	71
Reflective questions for the clarification: what's right for you	74

03 | Alignment: matching your business to you   79

The turning point	82
Your business model needs to match your nervous system	89
Measured growth	91
Be the boss	94
Accountability and expectations create shape	97
Boring beats sexy	100
Identify the people who value what you offer	103
Remember what you're in it for	105
Chapter summary	108
Reflective questions for the alignment: matching your business to you	111

04 | Interaction: dealing with others   117

Compassion first	119
Give them what they need, not what you need	123
Comprehension is different from communication	126
Tone tells the story	128
Always correcting can create insecurity	130

Gain permission before giving advice	133
Be willing to let go	137
Chapter summary	139
Reflective questions for the interaction: dealing with others	141

05 | Progression: moving forward — 145

Releasing value	146
Measure your step	149
Level up	150
Reframe discipline, engage choice and acceptance	153
Goal to strategy	155
Effective time utilisation	158
The lag effect	161
Succession planning – start early	163
Chapters happen	165
Chapter summary	166
Reflective questions for the progression: moving forward	169

06 | Acceptance: here we are — 175

A note from the author — 179

Preface
BURNOUT: THE UNWANTED BADGE OF HONOUR

In the world of small business, resilience is often romanticised. The sleepless nights, the constant pressure to grow, the personal sacrifices – all worn like hard-earned medals.

But behind the facade of hustle lies a confronting truth: burnout is silently eroding the energy, health, and longevity of many small business owners around the world.

Experiencing burnout is tough. It cuts a deep wound into the passionate business owner's mind, body, and soul. It can feel like a heartbreaking personal failing.

The good news is it's possible to recover from burnout, with more wisdom than you have ever had before. And if you haven't fully hit burnout, you can certainly reduce the risk of doing so by learning from others who have (which includes me).

BURNOUT AND STRESS FOR SMALL BUSINESS OWNERS

Across the globe, small business owners are reporting high levels of stress, anxiety, and emotional exhaustion. Reducing the risk of burnout is certainly possible, although not exactly straightforward. If it were, we wouldn't see these types of burnout and stress statistics:[1]

- **Burnout prevalence:** Approximately 72% of small business owners report experiencing burnout at some point in their business journey.
- **Mental health challenges:** A significant 88% of small business owners struggle with at least one mental health issue, such as anxiety, high stress, and financial worries.
- **Work/life balance concerns:** A substantial 80% of small business owners express a desire for better work/life balance. This highlights the challenge of managing personal wellbeing alongside business responsibilities.
- **Emotional exhaustion:** Around 65% of small business owners have experienced emotional exhaustion.
- **Impact on personal life:** Burnout has negatively affected the personal relationships of 70% of small business owners – a heartbreaking reality when so many start their businesses hoping to *create a better life* for themselves and their families.

WHY THIS BOOK EXISTS

I wrote this book because I know what burnout feels like – the silent struggle to keep going when something deep inside knows it's not right. The brave face you wear while everything quietly unravels. The exhaustion that seeps into your bones and touches every part of your life. It's hard on you, hard on the people you love, and it takes time – sometimes a long time – to find your way back.

---

1. Sources: Wifi Talent, Founder Report.

I've been there. And I've seen too many others caught in that same cycle.

This book is here to help you find another way – to align your business and your life with what genuinely works for your nature. If these pages help even one person avoid the pain of burnout and rediscover a more genuine, fulfilling way of working and living, then writing will have been worth it.

And I know it works. Over the past two decades, I've watched hundreds of small business owners make powerful, lasting changes by applying the same principles you'll find here – simple ideas that restore energy, purpose, and balance.

Kill the Chameleon isn't about complaining or catastrophising. It's about exploring a version of success that not only works in business, but also supports your health, strengthens your relationships, and honours who you truly are. It invites you to pursue growth in a way that's sustainable, balanced, and deeply aligned with the life you want to live. It encourages you to stop trying to be all things to all people or blending in with your surroundings.

These chapters offer more than just theory. Inside, you'll find:

- proven approaches to reduce the risk of burnout
- practical strategies to recover from burnout
- stories from real business owners who found better balance and clear business alignment
- a reminder that you're not alone.

Burnout isn't a sign of failure. It's feedback – a signal. A sign that your current systems, habits, or support structures need attention.

Burnout often arises in one of two ways:

1. We simply do too much, for too long, and therefore do not honour our needs.

2. We do too much of what doesn't suit us – with people or in environments that don't suit us either.

Neither is natural, and both are an attempt to deal with the environment by adapting away from what is good and right for you. This will never bring the best out in you, and can be damaging to your confidence and self-belief when you adapt for too long.

If you're recovering from burnout, determined to prevent it, or eager to grow in a more authentic way, this book is for you. You'll discover clarity and actionable steps to help you thrive.

For business owners, that means building something that doesn't just pay the bills. It means creating a business that honours your values, supports your nature, and gives you the energy, time, and freedom to show up fully for the people and experiences that matter most.

Imagine a business that expands your life, rather than consumes it. That's what we're aiming for.

This journey won't always be smooth. Life – and business – has a way of testing our limits. In those moments, I hope this book can be a steady companion, helping you navigate whatever season you're in. Even with all the insights in the world, there will still be difficult days. That's real life.

Reshaping and rebuilding can be challenging. Sometimes, it feels like two steps forward, one step back. There will be times when you need to do what you must to survive. But even in those moments, there are ways to ease the weight – and, in doing so, to gain greater clarity about what truly fits and what you're moving towards.

If this book speaks to you, use it as a trusted guide, alongside your professional advisers and counsel, and personal support team.

HOW TO USE THIS BOOK

You're encouraged to keep a pencil, pen, or highlighter nearby as you read. Whenever something resonates or feels valuable, highlight it and jot down any thoughts. You're welcome to write in the margins or spaces provided. Make the book yours.

At the end of each chapter, you'll find reflective questions. Some will feel especially relevant to you, others less so. Simply pick a few that stand out, and give yourself a couple of minutes to pause and think them through.

If the reflective questions feel like hard work or seem like a distraction from the reading, there's no pressure. Just skip them for now and circle back when the time feels right.

The more you interact with the material, the more value you're likely to unlock. This book is here not just to inspire, challenge, and guide you – but to help you turn those insights into meaningful change in your business and your life.

Introduction
WHEN SUCCESS STOPS FEELING GOOD

I had no idea my body had been trying to talk to me, my emotions as well. I didn't hear any of the insightful messages that were being presented on a daily basis. How could I? I was too busy trying to be successful.

Until I had no choice.

THE DOWNWARD SPIRAL

I felt terribly tired, and sad, deeply sad, to the point I could hardly function.

And had no idea how I ended up like that.

I had earnestly followed society's guidelines – I had a good job, earned more than I spent, had purchased a nice house, in a nice neighbourhood, had genuine friends and a remarkably loving and kind partner. I was physically fit and ate well.

This was the formula for success, and such success would deliver happiness. According to what I had come to believe anyway.

All the boxes were ticked – but there was a deep, overwhelming sadness. My energy levels were beyond flat. I struggled to look people in the eye as I was afraid the darkness I was experiencing might be contagious. I wouldn't wish the way I was feeling on anyone.

Something had gone drastically wrong, and it didn't make sense. Logic was a tool I had used to understand things, but it wasn't helping here.

Not understanding such emotions, I sought mechanical answers. I thought I must have had an illness of some sort. Glandular fever, perhaps. I went to the doctor, who ordered blood tests. A few days later, still feeling the heart-emptying depths of sorrow, I received a phone call from the doctor's surgery: 'You're a picture of good health.' They thought it was good news, and it was in one way – but in another, I still had no explanation for the way I was feeling.

I sank deeper.

The next step in an attempt to resolve this feeling was a step I didn't want to take. Regardless, I knew what I now needed to do.

It was hard. So much was going to be put on the line if I went through with it. But when your mental and emotional health is so low, life isn't really offering many choices. It was more a case of doing whatever needed to be done in a hope to reclaim my sanity.

I drafted my resignation letter.

I turned up at work the next day and submitted it.

In contrast to what difficulties someone may face in life, this was small, but for whatever reason my mind made it huge. In that moment, it felt like my soul was being gouged, wrenched, and ripped.

It felt like failure. A deep, sombre defeat. Something which was in stark opposition to fulfilling the conditioned idea of never giving up and seeing a project through to completion – grit, perseverance, and resilience – for these are the measure of a man. Right?

This contrast left me feeling weak, of meagre value, a drain on society. The unspoken embarrassment created a weight behind my eyes. It felt so very lonely, even shameful.

I was in a deep internal hole with no idea how I got there, or how to get out.

I had followed all the guidance of society, and ended up feeling terribly isolated from society. Even the people closest to me were unable to truly connect with me, or me with them. I assumed this was what depression felt like. But couldn't be sure. All I knew was the emotions, feelings, and state of mind were terribly hard to handle – dark, deep, distant.

My boss couldn't make much sense of my resignation, but he didn't put up much of a fight; he could tell I was done. Thankfully, he let me pack up my gear and head home pretty much straight away.

My wife was very worried about me. It hurts to be the source of suffering for another, especially when you don't know how to alleviate it. I didn't want her to worry, but I didn't know how to fix it. I was a broken man.

A day or two later, I was home alone with nothing to do, nowhere to go. My once light and easygoing personality had been transformed into the devil's dark. I lay on the floor in the dimly lit loungeroom. Arms and legs out wide. Not a single worldly responsibility to fulfil in that moment. And no worldly aspirations either. My identity had been stripped. I was an empty shell.

A Bob Marley song came onto the radio – 'Three little birds' – 'don't worry, about a thing, 'cause every little thing, is gunna be alright; don't worry, about a thing, 'cause every little thing, is gunna be alright.'

It repeated over and over. While I didn't believe 'every little thing was gunna be alright', I had no energy to fight against the idea either.

In that moment, with a yielding exhale, I gave up the fight.

Not the fight for life, I gave up the fight against it, against anything. I had no energy left to fight the darkness or the despair, or the other exhausting emotions that were being felt. I had no energy to fight to get my shattered identity back. I just surrendered – to the way I felt, to my past, to now, to everything. I gave no more energy to the activities of my mind.

I was done. Finished.

With that, a single tear slipped down the side of my face, my mind thoughtless.

And then. A sliver of space, or something like that. In that space, for the first time in a long, long time, maybe forever, there was also a sliver of peace. Peace – not success, not happiness, not achievement, not gratitude – deep, deep peace. A peace well beyond our material world.

It was a life-changing moment.

The peace grew and then, boom, a plug was pulled. All that grey, and black, and bleakness drained away like filthy dirty water down an oversized drain. *Whoosh*.

The devil's dark was gone.

There was silence and vastness. Lightness. So light. Blissful in fact. A second tear rolled down my cheek.

Life had returned. Light had returned. I didn't dare move. I just wanted to feel this feeling with all of my awareness. Without moving my head I opened my eyes slowly, and looked around. The lens through which I looked was different. Everything the same, but so different.

I felt amazing. I stood up. My sensory awareness felt brand new. Rebooted.

Walking outside to my garden, I looked around – everything I saw was a richer, deeper green and blue, and more alive than I had ever seen. I was in a state of deeply connected sensory awe.

I looked at my garden through a new, fresh lens. I saw the nature of nature.

And it was overwhelmingly beautiful.

It was the same garden as the weeks and months before, but the lens through which I viewed it was remarkably different.

I just looked. And in that simple looking, I felt deeply connected and aware.

Out of this silent connection arose what I can only describe as a conversation without words. Some type of non-intellectual understanding, seeing, deep perceiving and comprehending.

I felt a real and profound connection, and liked it, loved it.

This feeling was such a contrast from a few short moments ago when I felt so alone, removed and different from all of humanity. When it felt like no one saw me, no one felt me, and no one could sense what was really happening within me.

The internal peace and, in turn, communion with the garden was life-changing. What had happened to me?

It would be years before I would understand, and even then only to an extent. But I now knew what was possible.

KILL THE CHAMELEON

My garden, and its plants, revealed what steps would be next.

Just as certain plants need a specific environment to thrive, and not all plants will thrive in the same environment, so it is for people, for us, for me.

No longer would I pursue what society tells me is a good idea, nor would I focus on what I'm good at.

> Now my primary focus would be to figure out what's good for me and engage heartily with that. I would accept there are some environments that are good for me, and some that aren't, and make decisions accordingly. That is clearly nature's way.

As I looked at the garden with a deep sense of love and respect, I vowed to look at myself through that lens too. No doubt I would be tempted into self-criticism again, as many minds are, but I would remember the genuine love which is possible between observer and observee.

I would no longer seek continual growth, but respect that, as nature shows us, growth has a tempo, and there are periods of rest, recalibration, and reset. I would be guided by the pulse of my natural way and deeply respect my individuality. No more following another's formula which is mapped for a different individual.

It was time to kill the chameleon and honour my nature. A nature which I had been subliminally taught was not adequate.

I felt like I had been reborn, yet still looked exactly the same. No one would really know how profound this moment was, but the rest of my life would be influenced by it. It changed the way I saw myself and everyone around me. It fundamentally changed the course of my professional and personal life.

It was such a profound moment and new perspective that I have spent the past 21 years learning about it. It has encouraged me to nurture my internal and external environment, always working towards alignment – what feels right.

The transition wasn't easy. I still had bills to pay and everyday material needs to meet. I still had to figure out if I would return to the workforce or find a different way – perhaps sowing and growing my own food. I had to figure out how I could interact with society while honouring my needs and nature. I was curious if all the skills and studies I had completed would go to waste, or if I could repurpose them somehow.

There were more questions than answers, but at least there was a deeper understanding than ever, thanks to experiencing both the deep, directionless dark and the brilliant, vibrant light.

I'm so grateful for what the garden and nature taught me that day. It showed me *me*. And it differentiated that from all worldly success, personal achievement, and other manufactured methods of identity.

It showed me deep and thoughtless connection, life, and love.

It explained alignment and suitability without saying a word, and it showed the price of forever trying to adapt to that which doesn't suit.

When I look at my life and business decisions, and help my clients do the same, I'm always drawing on the insights from this experience. I regularly look to help others deeply embrace their nature, kill the chameleon, and do business and life in their way.

WHAT I LEARNT AND HOW IT HELPS

Through reflection, I came to learn that there were three fundamental areas that I believe led me to burnout:

- I wasn't being kind or fair to myself in my decision-making and thinking.
- The way I was interacting with others was out of balance and misaligned.
- I wasn't working or living in a way that aligned with my inner nature.

In the months and years that followed, I reshaped my professional and personal life around kindness, fairness, and alignment. In the chapters ahead, I'll share stories and insights from that transition – along with how similar shifts have helped other business owners find their own balance and direction.

These insights are captured in the following chapters of this book:

1. **A new platform:** attitude towards oneself
2. **Clarification:** what's right for you
3. **Alignment:** matching your business to you

4. **Interaction:** dealing with others
5. **Progression:** moving forward
6. **Acceptance:** here we are.

These are the areas I work on with my clients, but not necessarily in this order. I skip around sometimes because I can see that some areas are already well developed.

Similarly, you can use this book in a sequential way, moving from one chapter to the next; however, if you're already comfortable with certain areas, you can certainly skip to the section you feel most curious about or drawn to.

01

A NEW PLATFORM: ATTITUDE TOWARDS ONESELF

When I deeply accept the nature of the plant in front of me, my focus isn't about making it a different plant from what it is. It's already magnificent. I look after it according to its needs.

Burnout often stems from an inadequate level of respect, care, and consideration for oneself. I see it regularly – people kindly saying yes to anyone and everyone in the pursuit of 'doing the right thing' and building a business.

The intention is noble, and lovely in concept. However, the cost is usually high.

Through this sacrificial approach, business owners are often neglecting their own needs, and missing the signs that indicate they are either overdoing it or doing the wrong things altogether.

It might seem unusual, but in my experience, the first and most powerful place to start thriving and reducing burnout risk is examining our attitude towards ourselves. I've seen time and again that this inner relationship isn't just a contributing factor – it's often the underlying driver behind both burnout and the repeated patterns that pull small business owners back into that state.

While the advice to 'be more self-respectful' sounds simple, the reality is far more complex. That shift is often tangled in long-standing beliefs and deeply ingrained habits, shaped over many years. This section will provide an enquiry into different ways of thinking about ourselves and how we can be more respectful, kinder and fairer. We'll look at how to develop this in light of different situations that can often arise for the small business owner.

We start with giving ourselves the same attitudinal respect we would give someone we love dearly. We start with compassion.

COMPASSION FIRST

'Maybe it's about time you're more selfish.' These were the words I shared with a client who was finally succumbing to a business model which had burnt him out.

He didn't like the suggestion. Selfish was a characteristic he opposed; he saw it as something bad, something negative.

With this belief, he had formed the habit of running around trying to be all things to all people, without genuine regard for his own wellbeing. This approach was creating a lot of problems.

His stress was through the roof, and I was genuinely and deeply worried about him. After all, what's the point of business success if it puts you in an early grave?

It was an issue. It was like looking in the mirror from my own burnout experience from years earlier.

A complete business restructure was necessary, and that was a sizeable undertaking. To be able to navigate that, we needed to clean up his attitude towards himself first. His internal dialogue was one of pushing hard, and he expected everyone else to do the same. But few could really keep up with him.

The irony was he had a huge heart, a sensitive one too. He was upset easily. He cared so much. *Too much.*

But his mind was deeply conditioned; it was dominant, prominent, and overpowering, and often took the lead. He would regularly say his people were his top priority, as was his peace of mind, but his behaviour said otherwise. The long hours and client-first inclinations showed his conditioning. His welfare simply wasn't at the top of the list. Business success was his priority, and the road was torturous.

I shared with him the definition of yoga: yoga chitta vritti nirodha. Yoga is the state when our mind is free of fluctuation. He liked the sound of this, but it seemed like a distant possibility, maybe an impossibility. But there was still something incredibly appealing about stopping the endless internal mental whirr. To just have a break.

> Imagine that. Right now, a settled mind,
> no longer restless, agitated, elsewhere.

The first step to experiencing this is not the achievement of goals or dreams. It's deep compassion for oneself: the kind that allows a pause, a stillness, a rest, even in the midst of unfinished tasks, long to-do lists, and all the things still calling for your attention.

He took a deep breath and saw the truth in this.

He had just stepped a little further away from burnout.

He came to accept where the business was at right now. There was a lot he didn't really like, but he was able to accept it. Sometimes people assume acceptance means we continue to put up with something that is dysfunctional. Doing so would lack personal compassion (and compassion for others, too). Acceptance enables us to attend to something without the heat, without the temper. It creates space, which is where clarity and composure rise from.

Many business owners fear acceptance, as they have come to believe that growth stems from dissatisfaction, and the more dissatisfied they are, the more growth will occur.

Dissatisfaction *can* be a powerful source for change and growth, but at what cost? Is there another way? When discontent never stops, when it's endless, it destabilises the very thing that our lives respond most positively to: a stable and clear state of mind.

> Authentic growth accepts where everything is at right now, and is also willing to make decisions to align our actions with what feels good and right for our nature, acknowledging that not all things serve all people.

When I asked my restless yet motivated client, 'Would you like to feel unsettled for the whole of your life?' he said *no*. 'I want to be able to stop, rest, and enjoy the moments with my family more. I don't want to be stressed anymore.' He was sad when he saw how stressed he'd become.

I said, 'One way to help is for you to realise that what you have achieved already is amazing. What you will achieve in the future will be amazing, too. And can be achieved simply because you care about doing a good job for people. That is enough motivation.'

He then asked, 'When the devil goes, will the angels go as well?' I said *no*. Where there is passion and compassion, the angel of success and progress will still be present, but the devil of endless restlessness will slowly but surely dissolve.

You don't need to be perpetually discontent or dissatisfied. You are enough. Offer the same compassion to yourself as you would to someone you love dearly.

Part of that compassion is knowing your limits. You can't be everywhere, all the time, for everyone else, without overloading your nervous system and hurting yourself in the process. Some people may be disappointed – but the truth is, you simply can't please everyone.

It sounds simple, but truly accepting that truth can be hard. It's a fear that creates real imbalance for many small business owners, and it's something we need to look at more closely.

YOU CAN'T PLEASE EVERYONE

I ran a workshop in 2009. About 70 people showed up – a big group for me. For the record, I get a bit nervous with public speaking. Always have, still do. Regardless, I went through with it and delivered a full day exploring the idea of how to live your life, and make your wealth, in your way.

Afterwards, I received some heart-warming feedback, including this message:

> *I spent last Friday with Matt and 70 others on an inspiring journey of self-development ... really not what I was*

expecting, but I'm going back for more. I also brought a friend of mine and she walked away with a new approach and attitude to her life – she hasn't stopped thanking me for the experience and the gift I gave her through Matt.

Amazing, right?

Well, I received another email – from another attendee, who said the workshop offered *nothing new*, added *no value*, and was delivered in a way they found *laborious and non-engaging*. A refund was requested.

It knocked me around a little bit. I spent more time thinking about the one person who wasn't happy than the others who found it very helpful and valuable.

I know people have different learning styles, communication preferences, and preferred ways of interacting with the environment. Even with this understanding, it's pretty hard to be all things to all people. And this is the key point here.

The same experience can touch one person profoundly, yet leave another feeling unchanged. It's a reminder of a simple concept: I'm not everyone's cup of tea. Nor are you. And that's okay.

Do the work that matters to you. Show up fully, with sincerity and courage. Focus on serving – not pleasing.

And when someone doesn't resonate with your work, wish them well and move on. Polarised responses don't mean you've failed. They mean you're being real and authentic. Even with great intentions, there's some timing, style, and resonance that needs to align to synchronise with another. But sometimes it doesn't match.

> Be kind to yourself and accept that you can't be
> all things to all people.

When this is fully embraced, you'll flow through business and life with greater ease, learning which environments and clients are right for you and which aren't. To honour this it helps to overcome self-critique and find a way to sincerely and respectfully embrace your nature.

BE YOURSELF

It can be tempting to be forever trying to 'improve yourself'. While honing your skills is important and beneficial, there's also a strong case for being at peace with your nature.

Using the example from the previous section, the unhappy attendee also suggested a list of people I could work with who – *in their opinion* – would make me a much better presenter.

I reflected deeply on this and decided, *you know what, this just isn't an area I'm drawn to pursue at this stage*. Maybe it would have changed my career if I had gone down the 'professional presenter' route. But something in me just wasn't interested. It didn't speak to me.

A younger me may have pursued this, trying to appease the criticism and 'be good' in the eyes of another. But at that moment, I was comfortable in me. I was happy to share ideas and reflections, hoping they'd be helpful – but I wasn't particularly attached to them being 'wow', or convincing people that these ideas were good, or being able to engage an audience through enthusiasm and excitement. I was interested in facilitating a process to help people become clear, grow their confidence in themselves, and live from that place. Firing them up through motivational presentations is pretty much the opposite of what I feel drawn to.

I'm a long-term builder. I'm not interested in short-term excitement if it's only going to wane in a month or so. I see it happen often.

Over the years, I've supported many clients who've come home from motivational seminars full of enthusiasm, only to fall flat a month later. When people make commitments in an environment that doesn't match their natural energetic state, those commitments can be hard to sustain. The resulting 'high-five depression' is the emotional crash that follows being artificially pumped up.

I have had to learn to resist the temptation of setting lofty goals in moments of excitement or external expectation. Sometimes it's really hard to draw the line. I remember attending a workshop where the facilitator invited everyone to commit to new actions they'd take afterwards. I felt uncomfortable being put on the spot like that. I have resistance to making hasty commitments driven by a burst of excitement, or to please someone else's expectations. I wasn't willing to make a verbal commitment if I couldn't believe it with both heart and mind.

So, I said I wasn't going to make any new commitments. I wasn't trying to be difficult or oppositional. The facilitator seemed disappointed and suggested I lacked commitment. I understood where they were coming from, but this wasn't the case. My commitment was actually very strong, just not to what the facilitator wanted me to be committed to.

Know yourself and be clear on what you can sustainably commit to. Because if you aren't, you can become caught up in others' energy and enthusiasm which may be misaligned to what really works for you. Don't try to be something or someone you're not.

It's important to recognise that not all feedback is created equal. Learn to tell the difference between growth that's for you and growth that's for someone else's approval or desire. You'll meet plenty of people who think you'd be better if you did things in a way that they're happy with.

> The real freedom comes when you stop trying to impress everyone – or anyone – and start honouring your own wisdom. That's what allows you to truly thrive.

You can certainly entertain external ideas, and by all means, invest in your development – but do it on your terms, in a direction that feels deeply aligned with what's right for you. Engaging in development purely to appease someone else's needs is like being a chameleon, shape-shifting to survive in the environment.

You don't need endless stretch challenges or obstacles to grow. Think of a healthy garden – each plant thrives when it's placed in an environment that suits its nature. Growth happens, vibrant and sustainable, in rhythm with its own tempo.

CONTROL YOUR TEMPO

There's a common saying in coaching and motivational circles: 'Diamonds are the outcome of coal under pressure.'

The implication is that constant pressure – on ourselves or others – leads to brilliance. That if we just keep pushing, and pushing hard enough, we'll eventually shine.

For many people, however, and possibly the majority, this mindset can be problematic. What starts as a drive to improve can quickly become a never-ending cycle of correction, critique, and a sense of inadequacy. You finish one thing, and before there's any sense of satisfaction, there's the thought *what should I have done better* or *what's next*?

Sure, that might work for a few high-performing individuals – but often at great personal cost. Many who adopt this pressure-fuelled mindset end up worn out, disconnected, or even deeply discouraged. There's rarely time to pause, appreciate, and breathe.

Constant pressure is seldom the path to sustainable growth – clarity is.

When you're clear about what matters most to you – and why – you don't need to be endlessly corrected or pushed. In the next chapter, we'll explore how to deepen that clarity, uncovering ways it can guide your choices and give you steady momentum. For now, the main point to appreciate is that clarity itself becomes an internal compass – something you can return to again and again, especially when life throws up hard decisions or competing demands.

I recall working with a businesswoman who had been operating her business for over 10 years. She managed a team of nine and had built her success on years of consistent output, high standards, and a deep commitment to growth. She was also a wife and mum, and gave those roles just as much of herself.

It worked – for a while. But a person can only push so hard, for so long. Her tempo was simply too high. She told me she wasn't sure how much more she could give before something broke – and she was right to feel that way. Something did need to change.

So we paused. We revisited her reasons for starting the business. We explored what she truly loved about being a mum and a wife. We found new appreciation for the life she had already created – beyond KPIs and daily to-do lists.

> And with that came a shift: she began to focus not only on what she wanted to achieve, but *how* she wanted to achieve it. This wisdom helped her control her tempo.

That single change ended the relentless cycle of correction and striving. It brought a gentler, wiser form of motivation – one rooted in clarity and aligned with her values.

The pressure dropped. But the progress didn't.

A steady yet assured approach was regained. The same approach with which she started her business so many years earlier.

When we operate from clarity, we don't need constant feedback to course-correct. We know what we're aiming for, and we know why it matters. That becomes our guide. Our filter. Our strength.

Growth is part of life and business. But it doesn't have to come at the cost of wellbeing, peace, or self-worth.

Knowing when and how to adjust your tempo will help stabilise growth, minimise burnout risk, and bring composure to the environment. Once you've found that steadiness, another layer becomes visible. Just as controlling your tempo allows you to navigate your actions with balance, it also reveals the inner tempo of your mind.

These inner and outer tempos are deeply intertwined. The environment around you – your business, your workspace, your relationships – and the environment within you – your thoughts, focus, and energy – are inseparable. Mastery of one alone isn't enough; sustainable growth requires attending to the tempo of both, giving each the care and attention it deserves.

ONE HAND IN, ONE HAND OUT

Every day we inhabit two worlds: the outer world of our business, spaces, and people, and the inner world of our thoughts, energy, and attention.

When we put both hands into the outer – business, family, house, community commitments – we can get dragged all over the place: mentally, emotionally, and relationally. We may get one domain of life humming along, but others often suffer in the process.

I recall catching up with a businessman who had achieved exceptional growth in a short time. His company had grown from $2 million to $5 million in annual revenue, largely due to his drive and the dedication of his team. This commercial success was deeply satisfying – he'd worked hard for it, and enjoyed the rewards.

But there was an unwelcome byproduct; he had become irritable. His fuse was short, his frustration grew, and his mind was more distracted. He became highly reactive. He didn't like this version of himself. This wasn't his natural state – he was just terribly out of balance. With compassion, he accepted he could be showing up as a much better version of himself.

The issue was not just the business growth, but the fact that he had been operating with both hands on the business, and had ignored his internal health and welfare. Until he put time into nurturing his mental, emotional, and energetic health, his business success could never fully satisfy him. He wanted business success, but he also wanted to be a good version of himself.

To make that shift, he had to start valuing his inner balance and tempo just as much as his business growth. He needed to keep one hand on the business and place the other on looking after his wellbeing.

It wasn't easy. He had become addicted to the thrill of the chase, and anything at a more measured tempo felt flat, pointless, or uninspiring. But he trusted me, and he knew that if nothing changed, some big and undesirable consequences would likely arise in his marriage and personal life. We agreed he would engage in activities that challenged his full-steam-ahead approach, where he could slow down while still feeling productive.

He started walking his dog every day, taking his time to enjoy the environment in which he lived.

It may seem like a trivial suggestion – simply exercising a bit more – but the real challenge was to observe his mental tempo as he engaged in these activities. There was a great temptation to use this time to catch up on phone calls and close more deals. But this time was for mental recovery, and also a chance to learn how to choose the internal tempo at which he operated. It was a training ground to decide whether he would be mentally at 100% or comfortable operating at 50% for a while.

We discussed how engaging in a slower, more relaxed activity created the opportunity to recalibrate back to a more balanced approach to success, and a greater respect for the non-material aspects of life – specifically, being in a good headspace so he could genuinely connect with the people he cared about.

The capacity to turn up or dial down our internal intensity and tempo is a skill many struggle with. Yet it is precisely the skill he developed through this everyday activity.

To ensure his motivation didn't wane, I reminded him: *the first contribution we make to another is not in what we do, but in the way we are*. What we do for another physically falls short when it's done with frustration, emotional distance, or disconnect.

Before long, he was back in balance. Business felt good, and so did home life. He and his wife both attribute this shift to saving their relationship.

> You may be winning in one area of life,
> but often at the sacrifice of another.

To navigate this, place one hand on your emails, phone calls, meetings, and decisions, while the other stays anchored in inner observation. Notice the quality of your thoughts. Track your emotional balance and availability to connect with others. Pay attention to your tone.

Use one hand for contentment, acceptance, and peace, and the other for growth, ambition, and progress. They may seem like opposites, but in reality, they work together.

When both hands are used in harmony, something shifts. You begin to notice how your presence touches not just your business, but your relationships, conversations, and the everyday moments that truly matter.

Balance isn't only about allocating time; it's about showing up fully in each space you occupy. The steadiness and awareness developed through tending to your inner and outer worlds naturally opens the door to a deeper kind of work/life balance – one where being present becomes as important as achieving results.

WORK/LIFE BALANCE – AN INSIDE JOB

There's a misconception that work/life balance is simply about splitting hours between business and home. The truth is far subtler: it's about how fully you can be present in each moment, whether you're in a meeting, having dinner with your family, or simply listening to a friend.

> Presence is the currency of connection – without it, simply having the time isn't enough.

A lot of people talk about work/life balance and the strategies that go with it. Exercise once a day, set boundaries, turn off technology – these are common suggestions. I certainly recommend these and many others, but it's important to keep the bigger picture in mind.

Deep and meaningful work/life balance is elusive, largely because of the nature of our thinking – especially our imagination. While imagination is a wonderful faculty, the real challenge is being able to have a conversation, watch a movie, take a break, or exercise, without the intrusion of other thoughts, particularly business-related thinking. Achieving this level of presence is the holy grail of work/life balance.

In other words, genuine and nourishing work/life balance is not just a balance of external activities; it's a balance of internal mental activities too. Achieving this balance is not easy, and is especially difficult for independent thinkers and ambitious business owners.

I recall working with a successful business owner who had grown a sizeable business and was deeply engaged with their community. They were physically active and fit, and had the flexibility to spend time with their kids. They wondered what was left to put effort into. The reality was they were mentally restless. They looked like they had work/life balance and were successful in many people's measures, but their mental balance was lacking.

The next opportunity in life wasn't worldly success, but coming into connection with themselves, not as an achieving and motivated individual, but as a settled, grounded, and present spouse. They loved their partner dearly, yet when they had a conversation, their mind would wander to thinking about business or other productive activity they could do.

This restless conditioning sat deep. They weren't in control of their mental activities. Their mind was the boss and they didn't have a hold on it.

Their distracted mind today was an outcome of the past, and its capacity to focus and concentrate was something they hadn't worked on. They shared that they were able to concentrate but only when under demand, when a problem was complex, or when training hard.

What they struggled with was being able to concentrate at the same time as being relaxed. To be at ease and focused was a foreign concept and an ability they had not yet developed.

This aspect of work/life balance was going to be a bigger challenge than scheduling their diary or mixing business commitments and personal interests. Yet it had the promise of offering life-changing rewards.

My client is not alone. We see the challenge of this in everyday life, for so many people. You may block out time to go to dinner with your spouse, or catch up with a friend, only to cancel at the last minute because an urgent business matter comes up. That's not about poor planning – it's about internal priorities. When business holds the top spot internally, your external behaviours will naturally reflect that. Or you do make it to dinner, but your mind is elsewhere.

This is the subtle truth: while the practicalities of work/life balance are helpful, what really counts is how balanced we are on the inside.

> Our inner and outer tempos are deeply intertwined.
> The environment around you and the environment within you influence each other greatly.

You can spend a lifetime trying to perfect your schedule, but if your internal compass always points to business first, no strategy will make you feel truly present or fulfilled. This isn't about self-judgement – it's about self-awareness. And that's the real lever for change.

If you can build a balanced inner posture, the outer behaviours often take care of themselves. When you're with your spouse, you're actually *with* your spouse. Same goes for your kids, your friends, and even strangers.

By all means, use the practical strategies of work/life balance – but build them on a foundation of inner clarity and focus. That's when work/life balance stops being a diary-based juggling act and starts becoming a way of living, and being.

What we've explored so far – cultivating deep compassion for yourself, letting go of the need to be everything for everyone, and finding a balanced inner and outer tempo – provides a strong platform for this shift. These practices create the conditions for steadiness, presence, and a more intentional approach to both life and business.

When you desire to work on these capacities – a present and steady mind, balance, and composure – you're likely to come across the ancient practice of meditation.

At first, meditation can feel challenging or even uncomfortable, as it involves simply observing the activity of the mind. Yet it is precisely this observation – watching the mind in motion – that can reveal how our thoughts shape our experience and offer insight into their effect on the quality of our business and life.

Exploring meditation in this way allows us to observe the mind's activity, not as a task to be mastered, but as an opportunity to notice how we have become conditioned to think, focus, and react – setting the stage for a deeper understanding of how our inner world shapes so much of what we choose to do, and how we choose to do it.

MEDITATION TO MEDIATION

A lot of people who've tried meditation will say something like, 'I'm terrible at it'. That usually comes from the belief that meditation means having no thoughts at all – which is both unrealistic and, frankly, a little funny. After all, the mind's job is to think.

A truly thoughtless mind is rare. But a mind that pauses its constant fluctuations – even briefly – is possible. In fact, it happens more often than you realise; we just don't notice.

One of the most valuable outcomes of meditation is simply becoming aware of how active your mind really is. An active mind isn't failure. The awareness itself is the gift.

When life moves fast, we can't see what we're thinking. We run on autopilot, guided by old, conditioned thought patterns – many of which aren't even ours, but borrowed from upbringing, society, and the environments we've experienced.

Slowing down gives us the chance to observe our thoughts – not judge them, follow them, or identify with them, but just observe. This creates space between us and our thinking, and in that space, quiet transformation can begin.

Of course, what sounds simple can sometimes be complex, especially if you have thought patterns shaped by past trauma or intense phobias. If you're experiencing persistent or debilitating thoughts, reaching out for professional support is strongly recommended.

In many cases, though, the weeds of the mind begin to loosen as we grow familiar with our patterns. As we observe more and judge less, what once felt overwhelming often loses its grip.

At this point, we move from trying to be a 'good meditator' to something a little different: a mediator of the mind. The mediator doesn't try to stop or judge thoughts. They witness them with a little distance, and from that place can ask:

- Do I truly believe this thought?
- Is it helpful?
- Does it even belong to me?

This mediating space along with these reflective questions creates breathing room for clarity, offering a pause from the pull of habitual thinking. With patience, that space can gradually widen, and the mind can begin to settle on its own.

It's in these moments that we can feel the peace lying beneath the constant activity of thought. This isn't a peace we need to create, it's sitting, waiting, ever present.

Truly coming into contact with that deep peace can be profoundly life changing – just as I experienced lying on the loungeroom floor all those years ago. It's like noticing the quietness of the room when you turn off the TV. A silence that was always there, but somehow you had lost connection with. That peace behind thought is just like the silence behind sound.

While this awareness of both mental habits and the underlying peace is deeply valuable, it can also be unsettling. It challenges what many of us have been taught about success: that relentless drive is the only path forward and peace is the enemy.

It exposes the masks and mannerisms we've been conditioned to wear, the chameleon personas we adopt believing they are necessary to survive and succeed.

Years ago, I worked with a high-achieving client who had been a professional athlete at the top of his sport. When I suggested it was possible to be motivated while also experiencing peace and ease, he was both confused and afraid. His response was, 'I don't want to be a jelly blubber,' meaning he feared drifting aimlessly with the tides of business and life.

I reassured him that success and progress would still be his, but in alignment with what was truly sustainable for him and supported every aspect of his life. That conversation revealed how deeply conditioned his fear of ease and peace was – even though they are powerful allies when we value sustainable growth and our own health.

Over time, he learned he didn't need to be swept along by every thought to achieve or move forward. It wasn't necessary to analyse every idea his mind produced, and it was rarely helpful to be caught in constant thinking.

While it may feel foreign to an overachieving nature, it is deeply healthy to step back and rest in the peace that arises when you're no longer entangled in every iteration of your mind's activity.

As you begin to experience deeper mental stillness, you may encounter a wide range of thoughts and emotions, including less desirable ones like confusion or resistance. Sometimes it brings a quiet sadness – the grief of realising it has taken years to discover what ease even feels like.

As you read this you may even be thinking: *will I ever truly experience this ease?* This is a fear based in doubt.

All these thoughts and feelings are still part of the mind's activity, but they only hold power if you give them energy. Remember, our emerging foundation for minimising burnout is grounded in self-compassion. Observing even negative or uncomfortable thoughts without self-criticism increases the chance that your mind can settle again.

If you find yourself caught in thought patterns that feel unshakable or concerning, seeking professional support is a wise and practical step – and an act of self-compassion in itself.

A different person's perceptive can broaden our own perspective, and helps us see from alternative viewpoints. This shifting of perspective gives breadth to vision, and this breadth can be deeply valuable, further developing clarity and calm within.

IT'S A GAME OF PERSPECTIVE

A client came in recently. One of his admin team had resigned, and he was upset. He'd done a lot to support – made adjustments, acknowledged their efforts, gone above and beyond.

But they still left.

His first thoughts? *I must be a poor leader*, and then, *they aren't grateful for everything we did for them.*

We explored the situation. I asked him to look at it through at least three different perspectives before deciding whether any one of them were true.

Try yours. Then theirs. Then a neutral observer's.

We then considered the situation from the employee's point of view. It appeared they had been finding aspects of the role challenging, even with extra support. Their increased days off and visible frustration suggested the experience was taking a toll. They may have felt the role wasn't the right fit and begun looking for something more aligned with their strengths.

We called the operations manager to get a third perspective. He shared that the role may never have been right for the team member who resigned. Despite genuine efforts to support them, they hadn't been able to find their rhythm in the role.

These reflections helped my client see how subjective a single viewpoint can be – and how little it can be relied upon as absolute truth.

From this understanding, we could explore how the role would suit some people more than others. It was an obvious idea we had touched on before, but in this moment, it carried new weight. My client acknowledged that he had recruited hastily, simply to fill the seat, and learned a valuable lesson about the cost of misalignment.

This clarity empowered him to define what the role really entails and what success in that position would genuinely look like.

Instead of seeing this as a personal failure, he could accept it as a natural misalignment. Some roles – no matter how much support is offered – just aren't the right fit for some people. As he saw all the perspectives, his voice softened, his pace slowed. He didn't take it quite so personally. He saw the bigger picture.

This broader perspective empowered him to see with greater clarity – recognising his strengths, like his deep care for his team, and his challenges, like how easily he becomes caught up in his first reaction to an unfavourable situation.

He noticed that difficulty is often magnified from within. And with a calmer mind and broader outlook, peace and clarity are restored.

Interestingly, nothing had changed externally from the moment he walked in to meet with me to the time we were finished. But he was much more relaxed; he was okay. It was like his system had been reset.

A shift in perspective can have a profound effect. Simply seeing things differently empowered him to return to thriving – with authenticity, clarity, and positivity.

And that brings us to a common source of misalignment and burnout risk – not just for business owners, but for many of us: the fear of missing out. That subtle, ever-present pull can cloud our clarity, lead us to chase what isn't truly right for us, and quietly increase stress – often without us even realising it.

FEAR OF MISSING OUT

Fear of missing out – FOMO for short – is a term we often hear in social contexts. Maybe you weren't invited to a wedding, a birthday party, or a weekend away. But it's just as present in business: fear of missing out on a contract, a great hire, or an award at an industry event.

Living with FOMO isn't exactly healthy. At one level, it can reveal a lack of contentment – a kind of inner restlessness that makes it hard to fully be where you are. It can create a quiet hum of dissatisfaction that tells you there's something better going on elsewhere, and that somehow, you're not part of it. When we feel that way, it becomes difficult to be genuinely happy and at ease.

> FOMO taps into our desire for more, and therefore hooks into our insecurities.

It drives comparison. And comparison is the thief of joy. It can lead us to make decisions that don't actually suit us or our nature. I've seen this in business owners who try to mimic someone else's path – pushing for aggressive growth, chasing bigger contracts or high-profile opportunities – not because it aligns with their values, personality or capacity, but because it looks impressive from the outside.

The result of blindly copying someone else's decisions is usually stress, misalignment, and burnout. FOMO can lead you far from the very reasons you went into business in the first place.

Aspiring small business owners need to be very wary of FOMO in business.

I was in a business partnership a decade or so ago. We developed financial education software, and after a couple of years in the development phase we were ready to go to market.

At that time we were a fledgling business running on a shoestring budget, pitching to organisations 100-plus times larger than ours. We had some success with a few early adopters and from there managed to make some inroads into a relatively untested market.

It was exciting and unnerving as we attempted to build cashflow while at the same time pouring time and money back into further product development. Business would grow steadily, and then go sideways for a bit. Such can be the nature of new ventures.

Then a new and exciting opportunity arose. It was from one of our target clients who expressed a lot of interest in what we had developed. After several meetings they made a request: 'Would you build what you have built already, but in a new bespoke model just for us?'

It was an honour to be asked to take on a project like this – and, naturally, it stroked our egos. From a business perspective, it was highly attractive as well, promising regular cashflow once we moved into the development stage of the custom build.

As we dug into the scope and analysed the details more closely, the scale of the project became clear. It was massive, yet still intensely appealing. The work would look impressive on our résumés and could potentially open doors to more bespoke opportunities.

We priced it up and returned to discuss it with the prospective client.

They requested a few more changes to the scope, which was fine, questioned the pricing, which was to be expected, and seemed reasonably agreeable on where it was going.

However, something happened in that meeting that changed the vibe of the whole project. It wasn't something anyone said, it was a deep gut feeling of what was really going to be required for this to be successful.

To pull this off within the timeframe, we would have had to put our entire lives on hold. It would not only risk underserving our existing clients but also demand sacrifices in time with family and other important parts of life. In the end, we couldn't justify this cost.

We walked away from the opportunity, and revenue of approximately $1.2 million. At that stage we were turning over about $400,000 per annum.

It was a tough decision because we had a fear of missing out on the revenue, and the positive noise this project could have generated for our brand in the marketplace.

But we honoured our preference to do business in a sustainable way. We made sure we continued to enjoy the journey and look after what we already had, which was amazing and on the up.

Over the following six years, we experienced our ups and downs, but on the whole, growth followed a healthy tempo. We secured regular income from a portfolio of long-standing clients. The growth and product delivery were manageable and well-orchestrated. It became a desirable business for acquisition, and we ended up selling to a listed company for a rewarding price.

Sometimes I wonder what would have happened if we jumped in and took on that bespoke project, but I'm proud and pleased that we took the path we did, which perhaps many an enthusiastic small business owner wouldn't. We decided to take the road we felt was right for us, for our priorities, and with that, we still achieved positive commercial outcomes.

This example shows the importance of reflecting on our motivation when making any business decision.

In a slightly different way, FOMO can reflect a sense of entitlement. If we expect to be included in every opportunity, to be recognised, rewarded, invited – we set ourselves up for unnecessary disappointment. I've seen surfers frustrated at the ocean for not producing perfect waves, and friends and colleagues hurt and upset when not being invited to a gathering.

> If we can see that neither nature nor society owes us anything, we protect our peace, save our sanity, and find a calmer mind within.

If you can let go of the idea that no one is obliged to include you, just as you're not obliged to include others, you're free. Obligation is often a story told by the ego – it tries to hold power over us. But you don't have to buy into that story. You can choose something gentler. You can choose to trust that if something's meant for you, it'll arrive in its own time. And if not, that's okay too. There is always something else to enjoy, somewhere else to be present.

It takes self-awareness to recognise when FOMO is creeping in – and courage to pause, step back, and trust life more deeply. Sometimes you'll need to say 'no' to manage it, and sometimes life will be saying 'no' to you. By believing in yourself and respecting your own limits, you can navigate decisions with calm, clarity, and confidence.

This clarity helps us make better choices and resist unnecessary pressure; it also draws attention to another essential area of balance: how we manage the resources that support our lives. Financial management, control, and planning are not just practical necessities – they shape the freedom, security, and peace of mind that allow us to thrive. Which brings us to the next exploration: understanding the ways money can, indeed, support happiness.

MONEY CAN BUY HAPPINESS

Can money buy happiness? Of course it can.

Money can help us provide food and shelter, education and opportunity. It can help us share experiences with family and friends. It can provide comfort – more reliable or luxurious cars, homes, or holidays – things that feel wonderful in the moment and may even offer a sense of achievement.

But be careful: money can also set a trap. It's easy to fall into the habit of comparing our lives to the highlight reels of others. People's stories don't always show the full picture, but it can make us feel like we're falling short, that we should have more or be doing more. A quick scroll can amplify this feeling, but polished social media posts aren't the whole story. It's not uncommon to feel like you're not succeeding the way you 'should', especially when the lives of others appear so effortless.

At a core level, financial security certainly does matter. The stress of not having enough can absolutely weigh on your happiness. A lack of financial security, stability or control is one of the most common reasons for small business closure, and in these circumstances small business owners will often be on the brink of emotional and mental burnout as they try to deal with the stress that accompanies financial difficulty.

Accordingly, developing financial control is not just good business practice, it's also a commitment to one's mental health. It's an expression of personal compassion. So, take a step back and evaluate where you're at financially.

In business, be willing to analyse your numbers, work on your margins, and tighten up your financial control. Observe efficiency and inefficiency in how work is completed. Complete an audit and assessment if that helps. Meet with your accountant, bookkeeper or business adviser quarterly or monthly until you have a really good handle on how money moves through your business.

You can even enrol in a financial management course for small business. This is something I have seen successful small business owners do, which has given them more confidence around financial management.

> The effort you put into understanding your financial picture, and making decisions accordingly, will pay off in greater peace of mind both now and into the future.

With knowledge, you may realise some uncomfortable decisions need to be made, but at least you'll know what's needed and have the opportunity to be proactive.

I was working with a business owner recently who realised the ratio of admin support to income-generating employees in her business was out of balance. This imbalance was one of the key drivers of her cashflow challenges.

She's a smart, compassionate woman, and didn't like the idea of rationalising her administration team. We explored a variety of alternatives. One option was to grow demand and bring on another income-generating team member, but the real issue was one admin staff member was struggling to turn around jobs in a reasonable timeframe. This created workload difficulties for the whole team, and cashflow issues for the business. In the weeks that followed, this was addressed, with the employee eventually agreeing the role wasn't the right fit at that time.

The situation had reached that point because my client, being kind and sensitive, had tried to protect her employee by not calling out the gravity of the issue. Once she recognised that avoiding action put financial pressure on the business, and affected the business's viability as well as her own wellbeing, she accepted that change was necessary.

What this highlighted is that reviewing financial performance can open the door to sharper strategic planning and stronger operational management.

> Cashflow difficulty is a symptom and seldom the fundamental issue. Cashflow is the outcome of what has happened, or not happened, previously.

Cashflow challenges often arise from everyday pressures. These include delays in raising or collecting invoices, the weight of debt or high interest costs, and wage expenses that creep up unnoticed. They can also come from poor quality control, inefficient service delivery, or the difficulty of adjusting quickly when business activity slows and overheads remain fixed.

When we respect cashflow, we are also taken into a more healthy relationship with our business and life, such that we can get ahead of future stress and burnout by being proactive with our decision-making and activity.

One of the most valuable aspects of managing money isn't how much you have but how well you control what you have. Place robust controls around the activity that influences your financial stability so you can feel secure and at ease while picking up on the early signs when things are moving out of balance.

Ensuring you create the time to work on your business and not just in it is one of the key drivers to feeling in control, both operationally and financially.

CHAPTER SUMMARY

The attitude we take towards ourselves is a fundamental part of finding sustainability in business while minimising stress and the risk of burnout.

Put simply, when we genuinely and deeply care about our wellbeing, we're far less likely to overextend ourselves or compromise our core values to just fit in or adapt to an environment which doesn't really suit us.

When we place business growth or success above personal wellbeing, we end up saying 'yes' to roles and approaches which are simply unsustainable, and chase external wins at the expense of our internal stability. This combination often leads to chronic restlessness and depletion.

Many business owners have been led to believe that success can only come through significant personal sacrifice. If that belief resonates with you, you're not alone. Millions of people who burn out each year are driven by the same narrative.

I'm not denying that a sacrificial approach can produce results. But what it gives with one hand, it often takes with the other – in the form of strained relationships, poor health, anxiety, deep discontent and restlessness.

It's important to recognise there are many valid ways to achieve success. And one of the most important choices you can make isn't just what you want to achieve – or how – but how you're going to treat yourself in the process. If you're drawn to a version of success that doesn't require self-neglect, the messages in this chapter deserve your full attention.

Let's recap and summarise what these messages were:

- Treat yourself with the compassion and consideration you would offer to someone you loved without reservation. Challenge yourself, but do so with kindness and support.

- Recognise that the world is too diverse to please everyone. Honour your individuality instead of conforming to every opinion or criticism. Let go of the ever-adapting chameleon and accept your nature, while still working to overcome unhelpful habits.

- Find a sustainable tempo. Too little pace can reflect a lack of purpose or meaning; too much can come from desperation or unchecked enthusiasm. Balance is key to lasting progress.

- Nurture balance both externally and internally. Care for your business, relationships, home and community – and equally for your attitude, thoughts, energy and nervous system. True work/life balance depends on both.

- Use meditation – or simple self-awareness – to notice the tempo of your mind and the quality of your thoughts. This awareness can help you apply the lessons of this chapter to nurture your mental wellbeing.

- Remember there's always more than one way to see things. Considering alternative perspectives can bring insight, reduce stress, and help you think with greater clarity.
- Let go of the need to be constantly included or valued. Social media can fuel a fear of missing out, but accepting that you don't need to be part of everything helps calm the mind and focus on what matters most.
- Recognise the link between financial stability and wellbeing. While money alone doesn't guarantee happiness, managing cashflow and maintaining financial control reduces stress and supports health and happiness.
- No one can care for your wellbeing as you can – yet you may have been conditioned to put it last. Change that by elevating your attitude towards yourself to one of genuine and sincere respect. It may feel unfamiliar at first, but it becomes the foundation for everything else.

In the next chapter, we turn our attention to clarifying what's right and healthy for *you* – the version of success that fits your nature, not someone else's. This is where compassion turns into wisdom, and self-acceptance becomes self-direction.

You'll uncover what naturally brings you ease and flow, and begin to recognise the conditions that help you thrive without needing to bend, mask, or perform. It's the beginning of doing business – and life – on your own terms, and in your own way.

But before we take that step, let's pause for a moment and consider a few reflective questions to consolidate and personalise the insights available from this chapter.

Reflective questions for a new platform: attitude towards oneself

Below is a set of reflective questions inspired by the key insights from this chapter. *Choose three that resonate most with you, and allow yourself a few minutes to explore your thoughts and feelings honestly.*

These reflections aren't just exercises; they're opportunities to uncover clarity, strengthen self-awareness, and take meaningful steps towards living and working in alignment with what truly matters to you.

1. Compassion first

If someone you loved was in your situation, what advice, suggestions, or ideas would you offer to them?

_____

_____

If you offered more compassion to yourself, would anything change?

_____

2. You can't please everyone

When have you provided a good or service which your customer or client didn't really value? How did you feel about that experience?

_____

_____

_____

What happens if you consider this experience with a higher level of compassion and kindness to yourself?

_____
_____
_____
_____

3. You can spend a lifetime – and a small fortune – trying to change yourself into something you're not

Do you tend to be swayed by other people's ideas of what you should do, or how you should behave?

_____

Are you developing yourself for your own growth – or to meet someone else's expectations?

_____

4. Tempo

Is the current tempo you bring to work healthy and sustainable?

_____

If no, what would change if you focused on adjusting your tempo to ensure you have sustainability across the week, month and year?

_____
_____
_____

5. One hand in, one hand out

Are you bringing appropriate balance to looking after and nurturing yourself as well as your business?

_____

If this balance is out, what practical shift could you make to bring greater balance and alignment?

_____
_____
_____

6. Work/life balance – an inside job

Do you tend to feel balanced within, and what takes you away from this internal balance?

_____
_____
_____
_____

What really matters most to you in this season of business and life – and are you living in a way that reflects that?

_____
_____
_____
_____

When you make a new commitment to something which is important, are you able to honour it, or do you tend to let old habits resurface?

7. Meditation to mediation

Do your thoughts serve you in a positive way?

Do you think a lot? Imagine you could think a little less, even just for a few moments. How would that help you?

8. It's all a game of perspective

Which recent situation in your life or business could benefit from a second or third perspective?

What strengths do you overlook in yourself when you get caught in self-criticism?

Where might a broader perspective help reduce your stress or sense of burnout?

9. Fear of missing out

Where in your business or life do you feel the pull of FOMO right now?

Have you ever said 'yes' to an opportunity that didn't align with your values, just because you didn't want to miss out? How did it turn out?

Can you think of a time when saying 'no' led to greater peace and sustainability? What did you learn from it?

10. Money can buy happiness

Do you know your typical monthly revenue and overheads?

Do you know your breakeven point?

What could you do to enhance your financial awareness and knowledge?

What could you do to bring greater financial control in business and life?

02

CLARIFICATION: WHAT'S RIGHT FOR YOU

Different gardens for different gardeners.

Once we've learned to treat ourselves with care and balance, the next step is to look at *how* we do what we do – and the kind of environment we create around us.

Because even with the best of intentions, and even at a seemingly steady tempo, burnout can still creep in when the way we work, and the environment we work in, goes against our nature.

This chapter is about uncovering what truly fits you – the conditions, routines, and ways of operating that bring out your best rather than drain your energy. It's about finding clarity on what's right for you and trusting that wisdom.

To truly understand what it means to work in a way that suits your nature, let me use an example. Imagine I ask you to write – not type, but write by hand – a short essay on how your services or products help people. In your essay, describe your ideal client, what challenges they're dealing with, what goals they're trying to achieve, and how you would deliver your service to help them overcome their challenges and achieve their goals.

For some small business owners, this is a breeze. For others, it can be rather difficult because they're still in a process of developing clarity about what they're doing, who they're doing it for, why, and how.

If your clarity is still developing, this and the next chapter will certainly assist. The purpose of this example is not to test your clarity though, it's to highlight something else.

When it comes to actually writing the essay, you do something you probably don't think about. When picking up your pen, you're unlikely to stop and ask, 'Will I use my right or left hand to write with?'

Which hand you prefer to use is a deep personal preference that you simply don't think about. And using the opposite of this preference doesn't feel natural. You can still achieve the task of writing with your non-preferred hand. It may be fun for the first few words, but after a paragraph or two, there would be a strong pull to use your preferred hand again.

This is because writing with your preferred hand feels more natural and therefore requires less effort, energy, and concentration.

This same principle applies in business and life. Doing business in certain ways can feel good, right, and natural. When we go away from that, there is something that feels awkward and uncomfortable, and therefore requires a lot more energy.

There can be many reasons why small business owners steer away from doing things in a way that feels right for them. Perhaps they're not quite achieving the goals they seek, so they start to copy what they see someone else doing. Perhaps they've engaged a coach or mentor and just follow what they have been advised to do, without thinking for themselves.

Regardless of the source, this misalignment, in time, is likely to create a drain and make things harder. All of these 'little bit harder activities' build up, and then we start getting more tired, more easily. Using the essay exercise, writing the first few words with your non-preferred hand is not such a big deal, but a few paragraphs later, the task becomes frustrating, annoying, and just hard work.

Sooner or later, you'll notice your mind complaining – 'I can't do it this way anymore. Why can't I do it using the hand that suits me?' This statement isn't saying *I can't write*; it's saying *I can't write a certain way. I want to do it in the way that feels right for me, at a personal level.*

Same goal, but two different ways to achieve it. One feels right and has sustainability; the other doesn't.

This is no different for the small business owner. You may get to the point where you're thinking you don't want to run a small business anymore, but from my experience, this is usually more a case of *I don't want to do small business in a way that doesn't suit me anymore.* The same principle can be applied to any aspect of life.

The opportunity is to become clear about how to build a business, and do life, such that it deeply respects your nature.

DEFINE SUCCESS YOUR WAY

What are you building? What is your vision for the future, and what does that vision mean for the way you live and work today?

I listened to a podcast recently featuring a business adviser who helps owners scale their companies from $1 million to $25 million as quickly as possible. I shared this with one of my clients – an intelligent and capable woman who was once drawn to that kind of ambition and concept of success. But when I mentioned it, she squirmed.

She explained that while she once would have jumped at that challenge, her definition of success had changed. What mattered now was running a smooth, sustainable business without the constant pain of growth. She wanted her employees to feel confident in their roles and to engage in work that really suited them. She wanted her business to be set up so it didn't have its claws in her every waking moment. She wanted time with her family. She wanted a business that served her.

Every business owner, every person, develops an idea of what success looks like. Often, that idea is inherited – influenced by what others say, what society rewards or what we see in the people around us. Over time, we discover whether that definition actually fits.

> There are countless formulas for achieving success, and there are also countless definitions of success itself.

Until you know what success truly means to you, it's easy to get pulled in different directions. That lack of clarity leads to confusion. And without clarity, confidence suffers. You find yourself wondering, 10 years down the track, *what am I doing? How did I end up here?*

You've become susceptible to other people's ideas and priorities, making decisions that might look good on paper and make intellectual sense, but leave a hollow feeling in your gut.

One question I ask all my clients is: 'What are the five most important things to you?' It sounds simple, but many people fumble for an answer. Most start with family, friends, financial security, or happiness. Health sometimes makes the list. Mental health is often overlooked until I suggest it.

Once we have the list, we rank the items in priority order from most important to least. From there, decisions become easier. If 'time with family' is your top priority, working 80-hour weeks won't align. But if 'providing for your family' is ranked higher, that same schedule might make sense – for now.

Reflecting on this list of priorities can help us clarify what matters, and what matters can guide how we define success at an individual level. When using a process like this we can make decisions that align to our own nature, preferences, and values, increasing sustainability, suitability, and in many cases meaningfulness.

Drawing on the insights from chapter one, it also helps to maintain a compassionate mindset, appreciating that business, and life, isn't always neat. Realities like financial pressure or demanding careers often force us into misalignment through compromise. Sometimes we simply need to do what we need to do, but hopefully we can also develop a game plan so we can work towards a new model, one that fits better. The key is to keep the compass pointed towards what matters most.

One thing I've noticed: mental health rarely starts at the top of the list, but it often ends up there. When we reflect deeply, we realise that without mental wellbeing, everything else suffers.

I didn't see it clearly myself until I experienced burnout. When you come close to or hit breaking point and witness the ripple effect it has on those around you, priorities realign.

Today, my definition of success is centred on balanced well-being: financial, emotional, mental, physical, and spiritual. My priority list? Mental health, time with family, physical health, meaningful friendships, and financial security. I may not always express it in those words, but that's the essence of the foundation.

My outer life – my business, relationships and decisions – is now guided by an internal compass. My version of success is less about scale and more about alignment. Less about growth at all costs and more about being grounded, clear, and connected.

Take a moment to consider, *what does success really mean to you?* Explore whether this definition is something you truly feel in your heart, in your soul, or if it's just an intellectual model you've adopted along the journey of life. Keep in mind your concept of success can be heavily influenced by the culture you grew up in, and the one you live in now.

Once your definition feels true and right for you, ask: *am I making decisions that align with this definition?*

Hopefully, this little prompt can help you gain valuable and potentially life-changing clarity without too much confusion.

If developing this clarity is difficult, just keep reading and reflecting. I have found insights are always revealed to those with genuine curiosity and persistent enquiry. Understanding your natural inclinations certainly helps with developing clarity, and in turn consolidating it, and is where we turn our attention to next.

NATURAL INCLINATIONS

A plant will naturally face its leaves and flowers towards the morning sun. It needs no encouragement. People have natural inclinations as well. These inclinations can be common or remarkably personal.

For example, I have asked many of my clients over the years if they'd prefer to be happy or unhappy. I haven't had anyone tell me they'd prefer to be unhappy.

Some people say they can accept when they're unhappy, and this is actually a very healthy and aware way of relating to emotions. But even in these cases, when I ask, do you prefer the feeling of happiness or unhappiness, the response is still a preference for happiness.

So we could say feeling happy is a natural inclination most people share.

At an individual level, we have natural inclinations that are much more personalised. These are very important to recognise, understand and respect.

> These natural inclinations, when honoured, will make it far easier to make decisions about what is right for you.

To identify these natural inclinations, start by noticing what you naturally move towards. For example, if you enjoy focusing on your to-do list and find interruptions frustrating, then being organised and systematic is probably a natural inclination. So is the satisfaction of completing tasks and feeling productive.

On the other hand, if you have a list but happily abandon it when something more appealing comes along, then spontaneity and tactical opportunism may be closer to your natural way of operating.

If you prefer managing a meeting through a structured agenda, structure and order likely matter to you. If you're more comfortable letting conversations unfold organically, then intuition and instinct may guide you more.

For some, they're naturally drawn to mastery through repetition and refining the fine details. For others, new problems, lateral thinking, and learning on the run draws them in more.

There's no exact science here; your natural inclinations are discovered through observation and reflection. Notice what energises you and what doesn't. Notice where effort feels heavy and where it feels light. These are clues.

Certain activities, people, and environments will require far less effort to engage with. Pay attention to those.

I recall working with a client who felt lost in his business. He was doing a lot of general work in his trade to keep things moving. The jobs were familiar and profitable enough, but they drained him because they didn't tap into his natural inclinations.

His strengths lay in solving unusual problems and designing creative solutions. He thrived when he was mentally challenged, not when he was completing high-volume, low-margin jobs. He had assumed success meant growing a large team and doing more of the same work. What he discovered instead was that a small, specialised business, built around high-skill, high-challenge work, could deliver both emotional satisfaction and strong commercial results.

That insight has become a cornerstone for how he now designs his business and his future.

Interestingly, I have another client whose inclinations are the exact opposite. He loves designing business models around highly repeatable, low-margin services. He's energised by systemisation, scale, and efficiency. He's less interested in the technical complexity of the trade itself, and more about the thrill of repeatable growth.

Neither approach is right or wrong. The key is understanding your natural inclinations and creating an environment where those inclinations can thrive.

To truly embrace our natural inclinations, we also need to loosen our grip on the 'no pain, no gain' philosophy. If something feels natural, and even easy, lean into it. Yes, there will be times when effort is required, but let that effort be applied while drawing on your strengths, not fighting against them.

> When used in a balanced way, engaging with your natural inclinations has an energy-boosting effect, but not in a highly excitable way; it's more of a centred, powerful, and committed feeling.

To take this a step further, it's worth asking: *when you're free to choose, how do you like to do what you do?*

Asking *how* instead of *what* or *why* has a way of revealing the style, manner, and method that feels natural to you. Tying this back to the earlier essay example, we weren't focused on whether we were writing an essay or not; the value was understanding how we would prefer to write.

I prefer to think and talk a little more slowly when compared to many others. Doing so helps me be clear of mind and considered in my decisions. It helps me find the words most aligned to the essence of what I want to share. I also prefer to have a 15- to 30-minute break between client meetings. I don't have people lined up in waiting rooms, even though that may be better for the financial performance of my business. I do this because it's how I like to move through the day. Each of my clients gets a better version of me, and that matters. I also get to the end of the day and feel fresher. This helps me turn up at home ready to connect with my family. These are examples of my natural inclinations, and when I honour them, business and life seem to flow better.

My natural inclinations could be completely different to yours, and that's okay. What's important is that you identify what yours are. Understanding your natural inclinations helps you find the environments and tasks where flow is possible, so you can operate at your best without forcing or overextending yourself, enabling a truly sustainable tempo.

GETTING IN THE FLOW

Instead of success by muscle and force, we can look to switch to working and living by flow.

Don't force it; feel it – it's time to flow.

This may sound somewhat hippyish and new age, but let's just accept that there is something sensible about getting in the flow, especially when it comes to mitigating the chance of burnout.

Picture yourself in a river you'll be swimming in for a while. You can float with the current or fight against it. At first, pushing upstream might feel rewarding – the effort feels like progress, and the pain feels like proof you're doing something valuable. We've all been told that hard work means good work – that where there's pain, there's gain.

Then you get to a point of exhaustion. Or, in business terms, burnout. You can either swim to the shore, have a rest, and then jump in again and swim against the current, or choose to swim with the current, covering plenty of distance as you go.

To swim with the current, we first need to let go of old belief systems that tell us choosing the easier path is somehow wrong or less beneficial.

In business, swimming with the current happens naturally when we work with our natural inclinations, at a tempo that suits our nature, with just the right amount of challenge or intrigue.

If there's inadequate challenge, our minds tend to get bored. If there's too much challenge we go into reactivity as we're too mentally full. Engaging in activity that suits you, in an environment that suits you, with just enough challenge will help you lose yourself in the activity, bringing quality and focus that is otherwise difficult to find. When you're in full flow, time seems to stretch, energy feels abundant, and your mind becomes completely immersed in what you're doing.

While this is wonderful, it's wise to build in checks and measures to ensure performance is monitored regularly. Otherwise, there's a slight risk of becoming so absorbed in the immediate task that the business veers off course without you realising.

For example, I have found myself regularly in flow while writing this book. So much of it has felt remarkably effortless. It's such a wonderful state. But the process of writing provides no immediate income for myself and my family. Therefore I have had to break this activity of writing and book production, and make sure I still engage in other business activities such as coaching and mentoring my private clients.

It has been so absorbing that I have also needed to be conscious of keeping up my other activities, which are deeply valuable for balance, such as exercise, catching up with friends and family, and just enjoying downtime. After all, it would have been rather embarrassing to burn out from writing a book on how to avoid burning out.

Being in flow, and experiencing effortless productivity, can be confusing for many small business owners who believe greater ease means less security. Their sense of stability has often been tied to working hard, feeling stretched and stressed, and staying deeply involved in every moving part of the business. This relationship with business creates high dependency from the business owner on the business, which creates problems on a few levels, such as productivity bottlenecks and, at the other end of the journey, having a much more difficult business to sell.

Excessive demand from a business on its owner puts unsustainable pressure on the nervous system. In time, the business owner's mental capacity diminishes, making it impossible to be in flow. Developing appropriate reporting systems, understanding capacity, and having clarity on important performance indicators can go a long way towards rebalancing and recalibrating this situation.

For example, I worked with a business leader who had built his success through relentless hard work and personal responsibility. His accountant referred him to me, concerned he was on the verge of walking away from the business because it had become too demanding and exhausting. We explored delegating and sharing responsibilities, but he found it difficult to let go and continued to push hard.

The turning point came when we introduced clearer reporting processes and identified the key performance indicators that truly mattered. With reliable metrics in place, and an understanding of how these would be reported to him and when, his nervous system was able to relax. His mind found greater ease, and he could finally step into strategic management – working on the business rather than constantly in it – while also engaging in business development. Both of these activities were his natural inclinations, and he found himself back in flow and alignment. He could use his natural strengths in harmony with the strengths of his team and the support of his systems.

While business development and strategic planning really lit him up, about five years earlier he had looked after a different set of responsibilities and felt he was in a flow state back then. This is a useful reminder that what really engages you can evolve over time. That's why it's useful to conduct a review every year or two, or whenever you feel like business, or life, is getting on top of you.

You can start by asking yourself questions like: *which activities make me lose track of time and feel effortless to complete?* Then explore whether these are new interests or ones that have always engaged you. Consider how often you get to do them – day to day, week to week – both in business and in your personal life.

And always remember, what you find to be a flow activity might not have the same effect for someone else. In fact, what you find highly engaging and energising may actually be seriously stressful for someone else of a different nature. Deeply engaging work is always personal, and what you find draining and tiring is personal as well.

WHAT DRAINS YOUR ENERGY?

Once you appreciate that you have natural inclinations, and can recognise these, it will become easier to identify the activities, environments, and people you're not naturally drawn to and are likely to drain your energy.

> If activities and situations that drain your energy can be reduced, you'll have more vibrancy in business, at home, and in life in general.

Sometimes the types of activities and situations that drain your energy are obvious. You could do an audit: *what do I find highly tiring?* Write this down for a week, and there you have a useful starting point.

When doing this, you may find the types of activities you find draining are opposite in nature to your natural inclinations.

For example, if one of your natural inclinations is to be organised and reliable, you'll likely find it a highly draining activity to come up with novel and creative solutions if there's no structure or process. Or if you have a natural inclination towards kindness and compassion, you may find providing pragmatic feedback to an underperforming or misbehaving employee draining, even to the point that it dominates your thinking and affects your sleep.

Some people consider these draining activities, events, or situations to be their weaknesses. I don't really see them like this, but I can also see their point – they are areas they don't find as easy to navigate compared to others.

To be realistic, you're unlikely to completely eliminate the need to engage in some activities you find draining as a small business owner, and in life. However, the goal can be to offer respect and compassion to yourself and reduce the volume of draining commitments, and maximise opportunities to be in flow and engaged with your natural inclinations.

There are a couple of subtler points to remember.

First of all, what we find draining may have previously felt engaging. This was highlighted in the story above where my client found flow in operational activities five years ago but now finds them rather draining.

To provide another example, many years ago I started working with a business owner in their early 50s. They explained in their start-up years of business, the excitement of marketing and finding new clients was highly energising and engaging, but now that same activity was highly draining and required tremendous energy to think about, let alone execute.

These types of changes happen regularly for small business owners, and it's important to be honest with ourselves as we move through the different chapters of business and life, something we'll examine more later.

The other nuance to observe around draining activities is how a strength, when overused, can actually become draining. Let's say you're an effective problem solver, and you enjoy engaging in tricky issues and matters to solve. From my experience, people of this inclination start seeking out problems to solve because it feels good and they feel valued in the process. The catch is a few years down the track, these same people end up in my office complaining that all they do is sort out other people's problems.

In these situations, the skill, gift, and joy of problem solving, which involves the application of creativity along with logic, needs to be reduced such that we have a healthier balance of problem solving along with enjoying everyday business and life.

A sustainable balance matters. While most business activity is important, I often suggest to my clients that the most important task for any person who would like to minimise or eliminate burnout risk is to learn how to manage their energy well. That means not only engaging in energy-building activity, using our natural inclinations, but also managing energy-draining experiences as well.

Specifically, strategies like time-blocking can help, where we consciously limit how much time we're exposed to energy-sapping situations.

I had a client who had a big heart and never wanted to let anyone down. This alone can be a burden, but what was happening from a business structural perspective is whenever the phone rang, she answered because 'they may have something which they need to attend to urgently'. What this meant was she could never truly focus on the job at hand, which often involved reviewing and writing important legal documents. It was clear that her unchecked availability was going to lead to burnout.

We devised a strategy where clients could call, and if she had time blocked an hour to get some focused work done, they could leave a message indicating the level of urgency. As a result, we found there wasn't much that was so urgent it couldn't wait for an hour. We also managed to increase my client's productivity, which made her feel better about daily achievements, which in turn significantly reduced her burnout risk.

> When we identify highly draining experiences, we can use these insights to guide strategic planning with the goal of creating a model that genuinely suits us and is therefore more sustainable.

To provide a different example, I have another client who is a very sensitive person and has a natural inclination for forgiveness and always seeing the good in people. This had made some aspects of business management difficult and stressful for him, especially when it comes to dealing with disengaged, underperforming or dishonest staff members.

Unfortunately for him, he had a staff member who was being deceitful, and the matter needed to be dealt with. We needed to come up with a sustainable solution that worked with his natural inclinations, not squarely against them. In this case, an external human resources consultant was engaged, and a specific agreement was developed so he had support in an area where his natural inclinations were counterproductive.

This support remained a part of the business even after attending to this matter and is now a fundamental part of the operational structure.

This has significantly reduced wasted energy from worrying about something he's not gifted to manage, while still having expertise and capacity in place to ensure a fundamental part of the business is being managed.

Small business and life will always expose you to draining activities, situations, and environments. Even so, managing your exposure is important for sustainability and is an expression of self-care and compassion.

To further clarify what drains your energy, we can observe what elicits a reaction from you. This has the potential to deliver life-changing wisdom. I discuss this with all of my private clients as it offers so much insight, as well as the opportunity for some really quick gains.

OBSERVING REACTIVITY AND TRIGGERS

I often ask my clients, 'How reactive have you been lately?' Their answer gives insight into what they're dealing with, and how they're feeling within. When someone's anxious, tired, or flat, they're more likely to react to things they'd usually let slide, or have been dealing with things that aren't very agreeable to their values and nervous system.

We react to something we find undesirable, which we could call a trigger. Because each of us has different values, priorities, and old wounds, our triggers differ too. What sets one person off may barely register for another. Yet, some triggers seem almost universal for business owners, such as underperforming or ungrateful employees, cashflow worries, conflicting opinions among business partners, and unmet expectations.

It's natural to react to triggers like these – and it's important not to be self-critical when you do. But reactivity rarely improves a situation. More often, it amplifies stress and tension, not only for you but for those around you too.

That's because reactivity is hot, fast, and fiery. It moves before reflection can catch up. Even when it doesn't surface in words, it can be felt through tone, posture, or energy – the invisible yet noticeable vibe you bring into a room.

When triggered, our mental lens narrows. We personalise the situation, making it hard to see other perspectives. As mentioned in the previous chapter, expanding your viewpoint – seeing at least three perspectives – brings calmness, balance, and composure.

This creates a potential turning point from reactivity to responsiveness.

Responsiveness is cooler, steadier, and reflective. It gives space between the trigger and your reply – room to assess whether your thoughts are valid or distorted. This space is where real self-leadership lives. Responsiveness strengthens relationships and communication; reactivity strains them.

It helps to remember: you are not the reactivity. It's simply an observable part of your system. It's feedback – showing you something is out of balance between your inner state, your preferences and values, and your environment.

Maybe your expectations are off – too high, too low, or unclear. Maybe your communication needs refining. Maybe your environment doesn't truly fit you anymore, and your nervous system is maxed out from too much shape-shifting.

Reactivity can be seen as a teacher. It tells you when to pause, reflect, and realign. It reveals attachments – the things we grip too tightly – and gives you a chance to ask whether those attachments still make sense.

For example, one of my clients was deeply triggered by his fluctuating cashflow. One week he was cheerful; the next, anxious and irritable. His attachment to short-term financial results made it hard to step back and see the bigger picture. The narrower his focus became, the more frustration he directed at his team.

We recognised that his reactivity wasn't helping. It created fear and inconsistency within his business culture. So I asked him a simple question:

> 'What would change if you responded instead of reacted?'

That small question shifted everything. By choosing to respond, he reclaimed control. Together, we analysed what was driving the cashflow volatility. Some causes could be addressed – job scheduling, client confirmation processes, communication clarity – but these would only do so much, and increased acceptance around some cashflow volatility would help. Clarity replaced tension and his nervous system settled.

In this case, the trigger was external: cashflow. But triggers can be external or internal. They might come from a heated interaction or a nagging thought about the future. Some are major, others trivial – like your child's shoes left at the door, or another driver sticking to the speed limit when you're running late.

> Reactivity reveals where realignment is needed –
> in your environment, your expectations, or your
> thought patterns.

It also highlights your values. A flash of anger when someone questions your integrity? That shows how much you value honesty. A defensive reaction when someone disrespects your child? That shows your deep care and protectiveness.

So yes, triggers and reactivity can be uncomfortable, but they're also helpful if we take the time to learn from them.

I notice my nervous system elevates slightly when I'm running late. It's mild, but it's there – a cue that punctuality matters to me. Being in a perpetually rushed environment wouldn't suit my nature. So I plan to arrive a few minutes early. The 'why' doesn't matter much – perhaps it's about respect, perhaps calmness – but what really matters is honouring what is right for my nature.

As a result, I don't try to max out every minute of my day in commitments, yet I'm certainly focused on consistent productivity. Others are different. Some thrive in the adrenaline of tight schedules, while others like me prefer calm progress. These nuances provide insights into what kind of environment is truly supportive for each of us individually.

By recognising your triggers, you give yourself the power to respond instead of react – to choose what you'll tolerate, what you'll change, and how you'll grow. And if you're facing intense triggers daily, take it as a sign to review your environment, responsibilities, lifestyle, and thought processes. Not as a failure, but as an opportunity to realign your business and life with what's right and healthy for you, which in turn can rebalance your energy.

REBALANCING YOUR ENERGY

I was listening to a podcast recently, and the gentleman explained he loved to wake up in the morning and just start writing. He said he found it cathartic as it cleared his mind, ready for the day.

For him, writing is a natural inclination that energised him in a balanced way.

One of the comments I share with my clients all the time is, 'one of the most important things you can do is to learn how to manage your energy so you don't go too low or too high.'

Too low will start to feel like depression, and too high can turn into anxiety.

If you experience an energetic low, it can be helpful to move your body using one of your natural inclinations (as long as they don't involve overeating or overconsumption). For me, swimming, surfing, walking, and gardening tend to be my go-to practices to lift up. In business, I'm regularly energised through working with my clients to explore what's good and right for them, and how to turn this insight into practical business progress.

This is an example of how engaging in an activity with deep meaning and purpose can raise our spirits and energy. I heard a saying years ago that the antidote to depression is aggression. My interpretation of this is that aggression, a bit of fire in the belly, something which we feel genuine purpose towards, is a good way to overcome the sombre, flat states we may find ourselves experiencing.

On the flipside, if your energy is too high, you may need to find a way to slow down a bit, so pick a natural inclination that has the capacity to shift your energy down a couple of gears. I work with a lot of motivated clients who risk burning out from overdoing it, often through unbridled excitement. They are often at 100%, or fifth gear, as soon as they get out of bed. I encourage them to give themselves at least half an hour to ease into the day. They also benefit from getting a massage, stretching, going for a slow jog, or attending a relaxing yoga or meditation class.

Sometimes it's hard to engage in activities that bring us back to balance because we're more interested in doing more of what put us out of balance in the first place. For example, the fired-up, overachieving business owner will likely want to run a marathon at a personal best time rather than go for a slow jog, but this is just adding fuel to the fire. A useful analogy for balance comes from cooking. If there's too much heat in the curry, we don't add more curry, we add some yoghurt. If there's not enough heat, we add the chilli.

> What brings your system to balance will be
> highly personal, and a little bit of experimentation
> will be needed.

I was working with a new small business owner, and we identified he had a rather introverted nature, meaning that too much interaction and environmental noise was draining for him. He was developing a software product, leading to many days and hours without interaction with others. To begin with, this was a welcome relief from the daily interactions he was dealing with at his previous place of employment. This silence gave his system time to rebalance by being more relaxed.

About two months later, we met again, and I noticed his energy was a little flat. He'd been spending most of his time focused on his software product. I suspected that, despite his introverted nature, he'd withdrawn too far inward and would benefit from a bit more human connection.

He took the idea on board and experimented over the following month. When we next met, the balance of his energy had noticeably improved – he'd found the level of interaction that worked best for him.

It turned out to be a simple matter of not too much, and not too little.

Importantly, this balance wouldn't work if he spent six months with no interaction and then six months with lots of interaction. Balancing energy weekly or even daily typically yields the best results. I caught up with a client lately who was a bit frazzled. She had just worked 21 days straight. It was too much for her nervous system, and we agreed that daily balance needed to be prioritised again.

One size doesn't fit all, and it can take perseverance and reflection to figure out how to balance your energy. You can take hints from others, but remember everyone's system has its particular preferences.

This simple process may help. Start by observing your energy and rating it as high or low, then give it a score out of 10 – with 10 being extremely high, 5 a balanced state, and 1 very low.

Next, engage in an activity you believe will bring you closer to balance. Afterwards, reflect and score your energy again. If your score moves closer to the middle, you've found a strategy worth remembering. If not, try a different activity next time and see if that provides a better outcome for you.

I use the word 'activity' broadly – it could mean lying down to watch a movie, not necessarily something physically active.

Becoming aware of your energetic state and learning how to regulate it is an essential skill. It supports your wellbeing and plays a key role in reducing burnout risk and helping you to bring a positive and balanced demeanour to the people around you.

CLARIFICATION TOOLS AND TIPS

So far I have provided some insights with the goal of helping you gain greater clarity as to what's right for you and why honouring this is important.

Now I'd like to put some shape around how to make the most of the information that has been provided so far, and offer a couple of other tools and tips to help you clarify what's right for you:

- **Reflection through writing:** This book is full of reflective exercises. Take these exercises, think about them and actually write your responses. Writing has a way of clarifying and creating a deeper imprint about what you have become aware of. The deeper the imprint, the more available your awareness will be to draw upon in life and business.

- **Reflection through discussion:** You can also use the reflective exercises to inspire new discussions and in turn deeper insight. You can take any reflective exercise and use it as a discussion item to share with a colleague, business adviser, spouse, or friend. Before you do this, please read the rest of this book, as it will help with these types of conversations and interactions. I have found through my work that people are amazingly smart and know what to do in most situations; they just need to be able to work through it in a safe, supportive, and patient way.

- **Questionnaires:** I use two questionnaires – the Myers–Briggs Type Indicator and Values In Action questionnaires – with my clients to help identify natural inclinations, what drains and supports their energy, what are likely stress sources and what environments suit them. You can use any questionnaires you like and look into the results earnestly, but not so much that you lose the capacity to think for yourself. Some people assume the results from these questionnaires are either something to reject or something to hold on to without any independent thinking. From my experience, somewhere in the middle is most helpful, where results are used for reflection and consideration. When this is done well, we can arrive at remarkably valuable insights. Questionnaires can provide a shortcut to help clarify what your system prefers.

- **Suffering:** Suffering may be an unexpected tool to put on this list; however, it's a really powerful tool to develop clarity from. Suffering isn't nice, and I wouldn't wish it on anyone; however, it does provide deep insights when used with compassion and genuine self-respect. Suffering comes in many intensities. It can be subtle or overwhelming. It comes in many forms as well, from persistent underlying restlessness to intense despair, frustration, exhaustion, or disappointment. There can be an assumption that suffering is bad, and understandably so. It doesn't feel nice. However, suffering is just your system's way of trying to talk to you. It's telling you something is off, which may be your way of thinking, something to do with your health, or something to do with your environment and activities. Using suffering as a feedback tool transforms suffering from an undesirable experience into a useful resource to clarify what's good for you.

- **Joy:** On the flipside of suffering, we have joy. Joy is also the body's way of guiding us. It indicates that we are now in flow and engaged with life in a way that has a high level of synchronisation. This synchronisation happens when our mind, energy, activities, environment, and the company we keep come into perfect harmony.

CHAPTER SUMMARY

There is so much diversity in nature – and among people. On one hand, this diversity creates the rich tapestry of the world; on the other, it can bring challenges. This diversity can make it confusing to get clear on what is right for us at an individual level.

> Embracing our individuality isn't about trying
> to be different from others – it's about being true
> to our own unique makeup.

When we recognise that most people are drawn to the same core experiences – happiness, joy, love – we see that uniqueness lies more in how we express and pursue these than in the desires themselves. Still, this uniqueness is important to honour. When we do, we begin to shape the world around us rather than constantly compromising ourselves to fit into it. In other words, we kill the chameleon.

Let's summarise the insights from this chapter:

- Success isn't about living up to external expectations or inherited definitions – it's about what truly matters to you. Many of us 'try on' someone else's version of success, sometimes it will feel right, often it won't. These moments aren't wasted; they help refine your understanding of what's meaningful and authentic for you.
- Recognising what comes naturally to you is essential for building a life that feels energising rather than exhausting. When you align your work and environment with your natural inclinations and strengths, engagement and creativity flow more easily. This alignment helps you enter a state of flow, where productivity and fulfilment rise together.

- Just as important as knowing what lifts you up is recognising what wears you down. Some activities, situations, or people may consistently feel like hard work, and while you can't always avoid them, awareness allows better boundaries. Managing these drains helps preserve your energy and prevents you from running on empty.
- When your nervous system is stretched too far you may find yourself becoming reactive or irritable. This isn't something to judge yourself for, but rather a signal that your system needs care. Reactivity is like a flashing light on the dashboard, reminding you to rebalance before burnout sets in.
- We explored how to notice your personal triggers and how to respond before stress becomes exhaustion. Small adjustments – rest, movement, creative outlets, or connection – can restore equilibrium. Learning to manage your energy with intention builds resilience and keeps you steady through changing circumstances.
- When your energy runs too high, it can feel exciting, but often it's fuelled by anxiety or overdrive. When it drops too low, it's hard to move forward at all. The goal is to recognise these extremes and learn how to return to a balanced middle ground where you feel clear, calm, and capable.
- The final section focused on tools and strategies for clarifying what's genuinely right and good for you, rather than what you or others think you 'should' do.

In the next chapter, we'll dig deeper with our enquiry of what's good for you, as well as turn our attention to alignment – matching your business model to what truly works for your nature.

This is where the real integration begins: shaping your world to fit you, instead of constantly trying to fit into it. We're now moving towards the end of the chameleon approach to business and life.

It's an exciting stage – where self-respect and self-understanding become practical tools for design and decision-making. You'll begin to see how your unique rhythm and strengths can shape a structure that supports you – and how to help others work harmoniously in that structure too.

We'll be consolidating and deepening everything you've learned so far, helping you step forward with greater confidence and clarity as you apply your insights in business and life.

But before we take that next step, let's take a moment to consider a few reflective questions to strengthen and personalise the insights available from this chapter on clarification.

Reflective questions for the clarification: what's right for you

Below are a set of reflective questions inspired by the key insights from this chapter. *Choose three that resonate most with you, and allow yourself a few minutes to explore your thoughts and feelings honestly.*

These reflections aren't just exercises; they're opportunities to uncover clarity, strengthen self-awareness, and take meaningful steps towards living and working in alignment with what truly matters to you.

1. Define success: your way

How do you define success for you?

_____

_____

_____

_____

Has it changed over the past five or ten years? If so, in what way?

_____

_____

_____

_____

_____

2. Natural inclinations

Where in your work or life do you feel most naturally yourself – engaged, at ease, and needing the least amount of effort to show up well?

If you stopped trying to be who you think you 'should' be, which inclinations would rise to the surface most naturally?

3. Getting in the flow

What types of activities do you feel completely absorbed where you lose sense of time, and you need no extra energy to complete the task?

Can you identify where and how you engage in 'flow' type activities in business as well as in your personal life?

4. What drains your energy?

What activities, environments or people drain your energy? Can you identify what it is about these things that has this effect?

5. Observing reactivity

How reactive have you been lately? You can score yourself on a scale of 1 to 10, where 1 is not reactive at all and 10 is highly reactive.

How consistent is this level of reactivity? In other words, is this how reactive you are every day, or does the intensity go up and down?

6. What triggers reactivity

What experiences tend to get a reaction out of you?

How could you respond to this trigger instead of reacting to it?

7. Rebalancing your energy

When you're feeling a bit flat, what activities help lift your energy to a more balanced state?

When you're feeling a bit anxious, what activities help settle your energy to a more balanced state?

8. Clarification tools and tips

Using the tools and tips, and the reflective exercises presented above, write a summary of what's good for you, feels right for you and suits you.

This is a broad request and may be difficult for you to begin with. If so, you can leave this for now and read on. Further clarity often comes with a bit more time for reflection and observation.

_____
_____
_____
_____
_____
_____
_____
_____
_____
_____

03

ALIGNMENT: MATCHING YOUR BUSINESS TO YOU

When I look at my garden, my first thought is: what plants are going to do well in this environment? What type of plants are going to be happy here?

Once there's clarity about what suits your nature, the next step is to develop your business environment with this wisdom in mind. Everyone will have an opinion on what to do and how to do it, but remember they're not you. You need to be a bit selfish here and really respect what's right for you.

Keep in mind the first thing we looked at when creating a burnout-proof life was to develop a healthy attitude towards ourselves, and the first principle was *compassion*.

This is the backbone to building a business that truly fits. Your compassion for yourself needs to be high. You need to sincerely respect yourself; otherwise, you will keep compromising decisions to cater for a short-term business need instead of figuring out long-term sustainable solutions.

Shortcuts are not your friend.

In saying that, sometimes short-term tactical decisions may be needed as you look to navigate the complexities of business, but these should always be a short-term play while you build out a longer-term vision and design.

Let this design be guided by what's good for you, not simply what you're good at.

This may be challenging as we live in a culture where most people are encouraged to find something they're good at and build a career or business around that. While there is some merit to this, many people discover what they're good at isn't necessarily good for them.

We've looked at this in previous chapters, but it's time to squarely debunk this principle.

Instead of first asking 'what am I good at?', or even 'what do I enjoy?', we can ask 'what environment really suits me and will enable me to thrive without unnecessary strain or struggle?'

When I was bouncing back from my burnout experience, I went to a career counsellor. They gave me some questionnaires to complete. Most of them were fairly generic, with generic outcomes.

But one questionnaire resonated. It was the Myers–Briggs Type Indicator. Many people who complete this questionnaire have a quick look at their results and don't give it much further thought. However, I reflected deeply on the results and accompanying commentary.

For the record, I reported INFP (Introverted, Intuitive, Feeling, Perceiving). To provide a crude summary, this suggests I get my energy in an introverted way, enjoy exploring what's possible, am sensitive to emotions and consider the impact of decisions on the people around me, and prefer to be flexible in how I manage my time and commitments.

The report explained that these are all preferences, just like a preference to write left-handed or right-handed, as discussed earlier. It was suggesting what types of activities and environments I was more suited to, and would need less energy to engage with, and where I'm more likely to be in the flow. It didn't tell me what I was good at, but it was helping me go deeper with understanding what was good for my nature.

Just as I seek to understand what plants suit my garden's environment, this questionnaire was helping me understand what environment suits my nature. I was given the words to go along with what I was yearning to understand.

The catch was, with this newly developed insight, I couldn't see how I was likely to hold down a specific job in a structured company for any significant duration. My nature probably didn't suit stable employment as I knew it, and I would likely find busy and noisy workplace environments draining.

So in one way I had solved a part of the riddle – what environment naturally suited me – but created another riddle to solve – how am I going to provide for myself and my family if I'm not suited to holding down a job in the traditional way?

Interestingly, this second riddle didn't seem to worry me too much at that stage. I was so engaged in learning what was right for me, I was happy to figure out the rest later.

I then came across Martin Seligman's work on authentic happiness. This provided another message that encouraged my newfound approach: understand your nature first, and then figure out where to place yourself in the world.

When I completed the Values In Action questionnaire, a few patterns stood out. I have a curious and creative mind, and I notice when people are treated fairly and with respect. I tend to take a big-picture view, and I feel a genuine interest in seeing others succeed in ways that make sense for them personally.

This supported and extended what I discovered from the Myers–Briggs Type Indicator and other general reflections and observations along the way. It also reaffirmed that I had no idea what job I was going to engage with in the future, according to what I thought were my options at that stage anyway.

Interestingly, my eyes were about to be opened to what options really existed.

THE TURNING POINT

While conducting all of this personal research, I was also doing some labouring for a friend who had a small landscaping business. I quite enjoyed that. Working outdoors in the fresh air, using my body as much as my mind while still solving problems as we went. It was just me and my friend working on the jobs. Not too much noise, not too many people, nor others' emotions to deal with.

After a few months on the job, the property owners asked if I would teach them about personal finance. They knew I had a mathematics and education background, as well as financial planning skills. It was in my wheelhouse. Even so, I resisted. I was happy digging holes and learning about the needs of different plants and planting them where they'd be happy.

But landscaping was hard on my body. I knew I wouldn't be landscaping forever.

After about three requests to provide tuition around personal finance, I conceded and agreed to come up with something. In one afternoon, I designed a 12-part course covering everything from investment and tax principles to retirement savings and estate planning. I presented the course outline, and they signed up. Without realising it, I had just commenced life as a self-employed person, operating a micro business.

About halfway through that course, something happened to lay the foundation for my consulting business, which has been running now for over 20 years.

My clients – one a teacher, the other a doctor – didn't seem too happy in their work. They wanted to learn more about money so they could reach their financial goals, work less, and feel free and happy. The challenge was that even with better financial management, they still faced another decade or so before that freedom became possible.

I realised that while I'd helped them expand their financial knowledge, the deeper work hadn't yet been done. Perhaps it's idealistic, but I've always believed we can earn good money in ways that are healthy, meaningful, and sustainable for each of us individually.

With that in mind, I reshaped my course. Before diving into financial education, I began with an exploration of each person's uniqueness and individuality – what feels good and right for them. This shift brought my work into full alignment with my own values, and from that point I committed to making business decisions that honoured those values with conviction and compassion. It was then that my true life as a small business owner began, and I had a remarkably vivid feeling that this approach would become the cornerstone for the rest of my working life.

My first step with every client since has been a sincere exploration of their dreams and wishes, challenges and opportunities, their personality and values, and individual orientation. When done with honesty and compassion, this process can truly change lives.

The goal is simple: stop trying to fit into the world – instead, shape the world around your nature and what really works for you. No more chameleon.

> It means putting personal wellbeing ahead of simply doing what you're good at. And in many cases, that shift of priorities is revolutionary.

About 12 years ago I started working with an energetic businesswoman – a partner at a respected legal firm. She was confident, successful, and well-regarded in the business community. On the surface, she seemed happy and engaged. I was initially unsure why she wanted to work with me, but I've learned to trust that people often arrive with reasons not yet clear, even to themselves.

A meeting or two in we explored her personality and values using a series of questionnaires. What was reported seemed different to what my gut felt and intuition was picking up. My client felt the same way, so we continued to investigate, discuss, and ponder.

Clarity wasn't easy to come by. She had worked tremendously hard to establish herself in an industry with many traditional standards. It seemed she had adapted to be accepted and respected in this industry. I suspected she was finally reaching a point where she yearned more for personal freedom of expression than conformity to her profession.

Considering how much effort she'd invested to reach her professional standing, the yearning within her must have run deep, though she revealed it only in quiet, subtle ways.

From our enquiry into her natural inclinations, what drains her energy and what lights her up, we could start to get a sense of her nature beyond her conditioning. I won't describe this nature just yet, as I'd like the next transformation in her life to reveal it for you.

As her clarity grew, along with her commitment to work in alignment with her nature, she conceded that the firm she was at, the type of work, as well as the heavy commercial focus were no longer a match. She decided to resign. It came as a shock to many – family, friends, colleagues – with everyone wondering if she was okay.

In one way she wasn't; she had worked so hard to get to this point professionally and had to swallow the bitter pill that it wasn't going to be her future. But in another way, she was amazing. Her concept of success had evolved, and she was willing to make decisions that reflected this.

After she resigned there was a lot of work to do for a smooth handover and she completed this with commitment and honour, even though it was difficult as her energy was already moving onto what was next – at that time we didn't even know what that would be.

Following her exit, she came in to see me and announced she was off on a six-month trip to nowhere in particular. It was certainly an adventure of being no one, drifting around the world, with no agenda. Perhaps the breathing room she needed after so many years locked in.

On her return we picked up our work, and before long she had enrolled in a social entrepreneurship course and felt completely engaged. This spoke squarely and deeply to her nature and drew her interest in with ease.

She picked up a position with a local not-for-profit – still drawing on her commercial and legal expertise – but the application and benefactors of her work were now different. This lasted for a year or two, and then she could feel in her bones it was time for another move.

The next step was a much bigger one and involved relocating to the Pacific island of Tonga, where she volunteered for a charitable organisation. Her role was to support and mentor women who were establishing small businesses with the aid of microfinancing. This spoke deeply to my client and brought so much into alignment between her inner world and the outer. A couple of years later, she was intricately immersed within the community and found herself supporting these women, looking out for other community interests, as well as supporting the government to develop its foreign aid management – which once again drew on her professional background, but in a way she never would have imagined.

She's still living in Tonga today, more than a decade later. Many would say she's undergone an incredible transformation – and on the surface, that's true. But what really happened wasn't transformation so much as alignment. Being authentic became so important to her that she was willing to change her entire environment, to stop being the chameleon, and to make life, career, and business decisions that others might have seen as madness. Yet she knew exactly what she was doing. She was following a clear understanding along with sincere and deep feeling – she trusted her heart as much as her head.

Her nature valued contribution and compassion, sharing and fairness. She saw community as essential and believed in opportunity for everyone, regardless of background. That was her guiding light, and expressing this was her purpose. All we needed to do was help her find an environment that allowed it to flow naturally from within to around her.

Now, this level of change is probably too significant for many – including myself at this stage of life. I have a family I want to support as they finish school and university, and a move like this would disrupt that, which would conflict with my own values of providing steady and committed contribution. So, suggesting a change of this scale isn't the moral of the story.

> The message is that it takes courage to stop being the chameleon – to honour what truly matters to you, especially when the world expects you to be something else.

It *is* possible to find a way – a model, a rhythm, an approach – that's in alignment. Sometimes it's easy to discover; sometimes it takes patience and persistence. For the record, it's rare for my clients to leave their profession or business altogether. This story is one of the more extreme examples of change I've seen over the years. For most, alignment comes through smaller shifts – tweaking a business model, adjusting priorities, engaging in more fulfilling activities outside of work, or simply learning to think and operate in a way that feels more natural.

This last point – learning to think and operate in a way that feels more natural – can lead to a sense of ease and alignment that's just as powerful, without the upheaval.

About 15 years ago, I worked with an accountant and business adviser who learnt to hide his natural inclinations without even realising it. Like the example above, he adapted to what his industry seemed to expect. On paper, he looked like the perfect version of his profession: structured, methodical, organised, and logical. When we completed some personality and work-style questionnaires, that's exactly what came back.

But after a few months of working together, I sensed something didn't quite fit. There was a warmth to him, an energy, that wasn't showing up in the reports. So I raised it with him. We decided to look closer – not at what he *should* be doing, but at how he naturally operated when he wasn't trying to meet expectations.

That's when the real picture emerged.

When he was with clients he was more comfortable with, he was spontaneous and intuitive. He didn't need a detailed agenda; he followed the conversation wherever it led. His best insights came not from analysis, but from gut feel – from genuinely listening and responding in the moment.

We also realised that his need for order wasn't about control. It came from care. He didn't want to let anyone down, so he over-organised himself as a way of managing that emotional responsibility. His tidy systems were really just acts of kindness in disguise.

Slowly, he began to trust that side of himself. The intuitive one. The caring one. The side that didn't always follow the rules but often created better results because of it.

His analytical skills didn't disappear – they simply moved into the background, supporting the rhythm of his more natural style.

That shift changed everything. It opened up more honest conversations with his business partner and colleagues. They began to understand each other better, to see that 'professional' didn't have to look one way. It can be grounded, warm, emotive, and deeply human too.

Nothing in life is ever certain, but I believe this realisation – that his unique nature was already enough – has sustained him for years. He continues to work in a way that genuinely fits who he is, even when it doesn't quite match the traditional mould. And he seems far happier for it.

It took conviction and courage to make those changes. He risked confusion and criticism from the people around him, but when we come to truly understand what is right and good for us, it becomes harder *not* to honour it.

This story shows that working in alignment with our natural inclinations can create profound change – and we don't always have to walk away from the business or industry we're already part of. A few tweaks and adjustments can do the trick.

It is possible to feel like you can't make any change and you are stuck and without choice. While it can feel that way, the good news is that what once seemed idealistic has proven entirely possible: you can build a business that genuinely suits you and still be commercially successful. I have too much evidence of this possibility, which debunks the idea that it's impossible. It may not be a straight line, and may take some personal enquiry and bravery, but it certainly is possible to live and work in a way that is deeply good for you.

YOUR BUSINESS MODEL NEEDS TO MATCH YOUR NERVOUS SYSTEM

Over the years, I've had countless business coaches and advisers tell me what I 'need to do' to grow my business. But here's the thing – they rarely take the time to understand what actually works for *my nature*. Instead, they try to overlay *their* version of success onto my life.

But what's the point of building a business if it's based on a model that constantly stresses me out – and makes me irritable and difficult to be around?

The truth is, a model that feels sustainable and energising for one person might be completely overwhelming for someone else. If your business model constantly throws your nervous system into fight-or-flight mode, it's not the right model for *you*.

In 21 years of working with business owners, I've never met anyone who wants business growth at the cost of their mental health, emotional wellbeing, relationships, or joy. And yet, so many struggle quietly with anxiety, burnout, and frustration – often because they've adopted a business model that's simply not aligned with what's good for them.

So think carefully before taking advice from someone who's only focused on growing your business. Growth is important. But how that growth is achieved and its effect on you is more important.

> Small business isn't typically a sprint; it's a marathon. Accordingly, it helps for small business owners to be conscious of what type of business model they can go the distance with.

I remember a dynamic woman coming to Australia to promote an orphanage and school she had established in Africa. She was an impressive and inspiring woman. At one stage in her presentation, she spoke about the financial model and how much money she needed to raise every year to keep the doors open. I can't recall the exact number, but I remember thinking it was big.

The founder spoke passionately about her cause and seemed to have a great capacity to bear the responsibility she was carrying. She brought a lot of passion and compassion to her work.

A client of mine who was also at the presentation shared with me how impressive she felt the presenter was. I agreed. My client then said, 'I could never run something like that; my nervous system would go into meltdown.' I concurred, agreeing that I don't think mine would last the distance either.

It was a tender moment – standing in great respect for the founder of an amazing charity while still respecting ourselves.

As mentioned earlier, comparison can be the thief of joy, but at the same time comparison can help us reflect on what is good and right for us individually, not through judgement but through sincere personal reflection.

So the moral to the story is that not every business model is going to be right for you. Sustainable success comes from designing what works for your nature and having the courage to back that.

One of the areas I see a lot of business owners getting caught up in is having a model where the pace of growth doesn't suit them. Misaligned rates of growth have brought many business owners undone, often leading to intense stress, significant burn-out, and business failure.

MEASURED GROWTH

Big is better; faster is better. Right?

It seems to be one of humankind's loves – to build fast and big. We see it all the time; the largest building in the world is idolised; the fastest runner is too. I get it; new human feats are remarkable and grab our attention. There seems to be something special about them.

A few years ago, I undertook a major renovation. The builder was a young and dynamic guy. We were happy to give him a go. He seemed organised and keen.

He made a commitment to work on two jobs at a time. I liked this; it made me feel comfortable that he would have the focus to bring our job together in a timely manner.

Everything was going well until we hit the four-month mark. I came home after a day's work to find the foreman wasn't at my property.

I asked the builder where he was, to which he let me know he had moved on. This worried me immediately as it was the foreman who seemed to know exactly what was going on and when. His thoroughness impressed me.

Over the coming month, I learnt the builder had been successful in winning a few other jobs, and that they had commenced. Instead of the two projects at a time which we discussed, he was now managing about five or six projects.

I was concerned this growth was too fast for him and would impact our build. He didn't have the structures in place, nor the people management skills to hold something like this together. To use an analogy, he tried to go from crawling to sprinting, and in business, it's only the rarest of people who can pull this off, if anyone can.

He started dropping the ball on the basics. As a result, he needed to redo jobs as they weren't completed properly the first time. This cost money, which I suspected he was running out of. It became messy.

It reached the point where I told him not to bother coming back, even though a couple of things still needed fixing. I managed to find empathy for him and was able to part ways with respect and compassion.

What made this possible was remembering his intention. The builder hadn't set out to make life difficult; he simply made a series of decisions that compounded into a mess – stressful for him, his family, and everyone around him.

I've come to fundamentally believe that people do the best they can with what they have. What people have may fall short of what's practically needed in a situation, but they are still giving their best. Each of us brings a limited set of skills, experience, energy, emotional stability, positivity, values, and beliefs. Sometimes these feel abundant relative to the challenge at hand; other times, we can feel completely out of our depth.

Closing the work was a relief. I was tired of receiving promises that were often unfulfilled, and over time I began to wonder how much of what he shared was genuine versus an attempt to simply deflect another complaint. He was drowning.

We received communication from some of his other clients, wanting to go to the media to 'sink him'. I didn't pursue this; it's not in my nature, and after all, I knew his ship was already going down, and he was in plenty of pain and needed no more.

About eight months later, I received a phone call from an unknown number. It was my builder. He was deeply apologetic for the experience. He ended up using drugs to try to cope and landed in a rehab clinic. He had burnt out, and it took a very heavy toll. He was a husband and father of two. He was a devoted family man, and whenever he spoke of his family, his eyes lit up.

He called to inform me that his business had gone into liquidation, which meant I could claim the completion of any unfinished works against an insurance policy. He didn't need to make this phone call. But he did. And it saved my family a considerable amount of money and heartache.

This highlights the cost of trying to grow at a speed you're not ready for. The appeal of bigger and faster can be very enticing, but the cost can be heavy if it's not right for you.

If you want to minimise burnout risk, finding a measured growth plan for your business is critical. Growth can still happen, but make it a pace that enables sustainability and risk management. Gradually add to your overheads if needed, while at the same time check revenue and profitability are coming along with it.

Unmeasured growth is simply not worth it if you care about your own welfare and that of the people around you. As the head of the business, it's your job to control your pace of growth. But when you get busy, staying in control can be hard. Regardless, you must find a way to steer the ship and be the boss.

BE THE BOSS

I've seen it happen a lot – a business owner stops being the boss. Sometimes they are just swamped dealing with clients, or have lost confidence from a few business or personal setbacks, or have put in some management support and thought that would sort everything out.

They have ceased seeing the business as their work of art, their design, something under their tutelage.

When the boss stops being the boss, before long, employees, managers, or even clients begin taking the lead. Not because they're trying to take over, but because no one is clearly and confidently holding the wheel. When this happens, the business can start drifting. Decisions become reactive instead of intentional. The original vision fades. Energy gets scattered.

That's why it's so important to appreciate: if you're not being the boss, somebody else will be. I'm not talking about being bossy, nor aggressively controlling. What we're talking about is being capable of providing clear, grounded, and coherent direction. The kind of leadership which brings calm and confidence – to yourself and to those around you.

If you find yourself being pulled in too many directions, start by gently asking: what direction am I taking this business in, and why does it matter?

Take the time to develop clarity because when you're unclear, it's very hard to lead. When you're clear, everything gets easier.

Clarity becomes your compass. It brings confidence, reduces overwhelm, and helps you make decisions with intention. It also empowers your supporters – your team, your partners, even your clients – because they now have something meaningful to get behind.

Here's a simple metaphor that may help:

I was away travelling and trying to figure out how to get to a desired tourist spot. I opened up a map app on my phone and typed in the destination. It immediately offered four ways to get there – driving, cycling, walking, or taking the train – complete with turn-by-turn details. It could even provide an estimate of what the cost would be for the different modes of transport, as well as estimated times of arrival for each option.

Then, out of curiosity, I cleared the destination field and pressed enter. Nothing happened. Not because the map app was broken, but because it didn't have anything to work with.

Our minds, our teams, our clients, and our supporters are similar. They're likely to help you reach a destination, especially if there's something in it for them – but they need a clear sense of three things:

- Where are we headed?
- Why are we going there?
- How are we going to get there?

Figure out the answers to these three questions. Make sure they match what's good and right for you, and share them.

And then do something powerful: ask others what direction *they're* heading. Because leadership isn't just about being followed – it's about walking alongside, exchanging ideas, and moving forward together.

There is a risk, though. Let's say you set a vision, maybe even invite others into that process, only to find they have different preferences. In that moment, it can be tempting to compromise your vision to keep everyone happy. Walk carefully here – you may find yourself slipping back into shape-shifting and adapting, instead of moving forward in a way that truly suits you.

A few years ago, I had a client come in whose stress levels were through the roof. I asked him where he wanted to go with his business. His answer was simple, yet powerful: 'I don't care where it goes – I just can't keep doing this, with this level of stress.'

At first glance, that might sound like a lack of vision. But in truth, it was crystal clear – his top priority was peace. Everything else was secondary.

That clarity gave him permission to step back into his rightful place as the boss. He wasn't afraid of losing employees or clients if they were contributing to his stress. We agreed the business needed reshaping – a new structure that worked *for* him, not against him. And if that couldn't happen, he was ready to walk away and operate from home as a sole trader. He was accepting of either outcome.

It took time to develop the right shape and structure – something I'll talk about in the next section – but the key turning point was his decision to lead with clarity and self-respect. He began clearly articulating to his team where the business was heading, why it mattered, and what success would look like: mutual commitment to schedules, consistent focus, steady cashflow, and thoughtful communication.

From suffering came clarity – and through self-respect came change. It wasn't easy, but it was necessary. And it laid the foundation for a much healthier future.

> Chapters shift. Focus changes. And that's okay.
> Just don't give up your role in the driver's seat.

The challenge going forward is to hold the new shape and not drop back into old habits. For this, we need to communicate expectations and develop models for accountability.

ACCOUNTABILITY AND EXPECTATIONS CREATE SHAPE

I've often seen business owners fail to place clear expectations on their team – and even on their clients. Sometimes this is because they're not sure of their expectations in the first place, are too busy to have the conversation, or are afraid they won't be received well.

Regardless of why they aren't communicated, when expectations aren't clear, the business starts to lose shape. Things become vague, roles blur, and momentum slows. From there, it's a slippery slope into underperformance, difficult team dynamics, and unnecessary stress for the owner. You end up carrying more than your share, often without realising it – until it wears you down.

To avoid this, begin by clarifying what's expected and share this.

When I start working with a new client, we always complete an expectation-clarifying exercise. I ask 'what can I expect from you?', 'what do you expect from me?' and 'what would you like to get out of our work together?'

We would have already discussed the last point, but this process confirms and further clarifies it. Sometimes it comes as a surprise for me to ask, 'what can I expect from you?' Doing so is important, though. I get to find out if I can expect them to be punctual, pay fees on time, be open-minded, and willing to try new ideas out. We get to talk about expectations in a warm and friendly way and see if either person needs to bring something else to the table to help our chances of success.

By having this discussion, we form an understanding that we can use for future conversations if we need to bring something back into line. Interestingly, this is hardly ever needed; I think partly because we go through this process upfront.

I also get to check what's expected of me, and whether this is reasonable based on what I can provide. It's a really healthy conversation, and it helps with alignment and reducing the likelihood of surprises.

With expectations clarified, the next step is to be willing to hold some form of accountability.

Accountability doesn't mean being harsh or micromanaging. At its core, it means having agreed-upon standards, clarity around who does what, and open conversations about how things are tracking. It's not about pressure – it's about shape, rhythm, and shared direction.

I introduced in the previous section my client who was on the brink of serious burnout and had accepted that change was necessary. While he was working long hours, his burnout wasn't just the result of overdoing it – it came from trying to operate within a business model that didn't suit his nature.

He had a friendly team, but expectations weren't clear, and there was no accountability for basic behaviour or performance standards. He reached a crossroads: leave things the way they were and keep absorbing the stress, or introduce changes and risk upsetting the team.

He took the latter option because he was simply at breaking point from stress overload. I encouraged him to take responsibility for the way the business was currently operating. This may sound tough, but in fact it is liberating to do this as we realise we can actually do something about it. After all, it was a lack of certain actions that enabled the business to become as loose as it was.

We looked at the business through a few different perspectives and clarified what needed to be introduced. These were essentially new expectations to bring structure and order. This clarity, along with some other exercises to reduce his pent-up frustration, made it possible to deliver these new standards to his business with calmness, composure, and respect.

The result?

In the six months that followed, no one left. In fact, two team members stepped up and shared their desire to stay long-term. The newfound clarity gave them something they could commit to. The structure didn't push them away – it gave them a new sense of purpose and stability.

One of the other byproducts was a remarkable improvement in the financial performance of the business. This, along with a more predictable and reliable structure, reduced the stress levels of my client significantly, helping him sleep better and have better relationships with the people he loved.

He was at serious risk of burnout before these changes. The risk has been significantly reduced by clarifying expectations and bringing some accountability measures into the management processes.

It can feel uncomfortable at first to raise expectations or tighten accountability. But it's far more uncomfortable for everybody when you lead in chaos.

> Structure isn't restrictive – it's supportive. It allows your team to know where they stand, how they contribute, and how to succeed.

A genuine study into human needs reveals how important structure is to most people. Once a person is able to feed themselves, the next desire is stability and security. Some people don't need much to feel stable and secure, but most people actually need quite a lot.

Clear structure and expectations, along with compassionate support, go a long way to building a culture you can enjoy as the business leader. Such a structure will most likely work for your team and clients as well.

When you add a layer of accountability, you may find someone isn't willing to carry their weight for the team. If this happens, it's important to have a conversation to determine what they want, what works for them, and whether this aligns with how you'd like to run your business.

These can be delicate areas emotionally and legally, so it's a good idea to seek the advice of an employment and human resources professional in these circumstances.

Clear expectations and kind, consistent accountability help you build structure and control in your business without constant hands-on involvement. This in itself can significantly alleviate burnout risk and help both business owners and their businesses to thrive. What we put in place wasn't sexy, but it was the cornerstone for clarity, consistency, and commitment.

BORING BEATS SEXY

Sexy beats boring every day of the week, right?

Not in business.

Business needs the basics to work well. Without that, everything else rests on a shaky base – a bit like building a luxury home on swampy ground.

You can be the most charismatic, exciting, innovative person in the room – but if you can't deliver with reliability, consistency, and integrity, it all starts to unravel.

Interestingly, it's often the small, repeatable actions – the ones that feel unglamorous and even a little dull – that form the real foundation for success. The catch is, not everyone is suited to the continuous execution of the steady and repeatable basics. They're not shiny. They're not thrilling. So for those of us who thrive on new experiences (myself included), routine can feel like the opposite of our natural inclinations.

I once worked with a business owner who taught me a lot about this. He was successful by many measures – smart, driven, genuinely caring – but I could always tell how well the basics were being looked after within the first minute of our session.

To anyone else, he probably seemed fine. But I could hear it in his voice – just a little faster, a little louder than usual. He wasn't getting the basics right. In his case, it wasn't just the business basics; it was the balance of life's basics too.

His days followed a pattern: straight into emails in the morning, then hours at the desk. A quick break for meals with the family – and even then, his mind was often still at work. Evenings were more of the same. His mind never had a chance to settle.

He wasn't angry. He wasn't unkind. He was just stretched because he wasn't doing the basics well. Over time, his composure began to wear thin. He started to withdraw.

When I asked him what success looked like, he mentioned business success – but also being mentally healthy, a present partner for his wife, and a connected parent. He knew the last two parts were slipping through his fingers.

So we undertook a process to identify the basics that needed to be honoured and repeated for him to experience meaningful success. He started carving out time for things that didn't look like productivity from the outside but created calm and connection on the inside. A walk by the lake. A slow lunch. A picnic with his wife. Logging off early. Being fully in the conversations.

He also started to create a steady morning rhythm that grounded him before jumping into his inbox. He paid attention to his internal tempo and took action when it started speeding up. He gave proper time to joy and connection, not just output. And this helped him show up for the foundational work in his business – even when it felt boring – because he understood that this was what made everything else possible.

It seemed counterintuitive for him to begin with – getting the basics sorted outside of business first. But what that created was a clearer mind to think through the dynamics of his business, instead of covering up issues just by working more.

With clearer thinking, we could assess inefficiencies and where he was overthinking. We investigated whether the systems and processes could be trusted, and discovered they could be. They were excellent, in fact, but he was still learning how to let the systems and processes do the heavy lifting. To resolve this, we developed a little more structure, which at first he thought would be restricting, but with time felt more rhythmic and flowing.

Efficiency in execution improved, and his overthinking subsided. He was able to get back to clients in a more timely manner, and found he could turn around jobs with less angst and more composure and ease.

He discovered that simple can be good, and learnt that when the basics aren't being looked after every day, business is much harder than it needs to be.

While some of my clients can maintain steady, consistent execution day after day, for this particular person, that simply wasn't sustainable – it's not in his nature. He's far better suited to sparking new conversations with clients, exploring fresh opportunities, and analysing ways to grow the business. But as mentioned earlier, none of that is sustainable without a solid foundation. He's since built that foundation – sometimes you have to do what you have to do.

With this platform he was able to appoint an administration assistant who will further help with executing the much-needed basics that are critical. A function that happens to suit the nature of the new recruit, and with this development, he's free to work in a way that truly fits.

We now have both team members working in their own styles, in alignment with what suits them, in a collaborative way, with the basics of business being attended to, as well as growth and client engagement. They understand each other's strengths and respect each other's individuality.

When things speed up for the business owner and he notices he's being swallowed by his business, he catches it sooner and can talk through opportunities for rebalancing with his assistant.

Through this experience, he came to learn an important lesson.

> It doesn't matter how smart or clever you are; if the basics are being ignored or overlooked, sooner or later you will find yourself surrounded by chaos.

A good indicator of whether the basics are being looked after is how smoothly business and life are progressing for you, your family, team, and clients. *Results are important, but the smoothness of movement towards those results is the real indicator.*

The smoothness of your day depends on several factors. How effortlessly you move through your tasks, how well your team is developed, and whether you have the right people around you all play a part. Another key factor is the clients you work with and whether they truly fit the service or product your business provides. This last point is especially important, and it's where we'll turn our attention next.

IDENTIFY THE PEOPLE WHO VALUE WHAT YOU OFFER

So, my hot water system came to its death. To replace it with something similar would cost about $5,000. While I don't really like spending money on stuff like this, I do like the luxury of long-lasting hot water.

What's interesting is that about a month ago, I willingly and somewhat joyfully spent four times this amount on a family holiday to Japan.

So why was I so committed and happy to spend $20,000 one month and then begrudgingly spend $5,000 the next? Because the way we see money is subjective and psychological. Value is completely personal.

This reminded me of a friend I once invited to travel with me. He declined, choosing instead to invest the money in shares. I hope that investment served him well, but for me, the experience of travel was worth far more than any financial return. At that point in my life, travel held greater value – and that's where I chose to invest.

The same principle applies in business. Years ago, a woman enquired about my services. It seemed a perfect fit, but she decided not to proceed – perhaps because the timing or expense didn't feel right. A few months later, I saw photos of her enjoying a holiday in Italy, a trip that likely cost several times my fee.

I share this not to question her choices, but to illustrate an important truth: value is personal. No matter how strongly we believe someone could benefit from what we offer, they will decide based on their own hierarchy of values.

Our job as business owners is to understand this – to communicate value in ways that resonate, while accepting that not everyone will see it the same way. As one sales coach once told me, 'People who need a heart transplant somehow find the money.' When something truly matters, people make it happen.

It's rarely about price; it's about desire. Some people will never buy what you offer simply because it isn't important enough to them – and that's okay.

> Your task is to identify the people who genuinely value what you offer, set a price that reflects that value, and ensure there are enough of those people to sustain and grow your business.

Once that's in place, marketing becomes about connection, not persuasion. When you understand that value is personal, you naturally engage with more empathy. You stop pushing products and start aligning with what matters most to you and your clients – creating relationships that last.

Just like my trip to Japan, when we invest in what truly matters, the return – whether financial, emotional, or relational – is far more rewarding.

In business, the clients and customers who are most likely the hardest to deal with will be the ones who value your service the least. They'll be more likely to question fees, cancel meetings or appointments late, and ask for refunds. Those who deeply value what you have to offer will respect your time and expertise at a much higher level.

Find these people and business will naturally be smoother, and you'll be much less tempted to shape shift like the chameleon to appease those who don't suit you. You may find this doesn't just apply in business domains, but can also apply in your personal life.

To achieve this in business, it helps to be crystal clear as to why you went into it in the first place.

REMEMBER WHAT YOU'RE IN IT FOR

Many business owners I've worked with tell me they went into business for flexibility and lifestyle. What a lovely idea. And yes – business *can* deliver this. But more often than not, it leads us down one of countless other rabbit holes.

That's why it's worth regularly pausing to remember: *what did I get into this for? And is this how I thought it would be?*

If your goal is to make as much money as possible, there's a good chance you're in the wrong industry – and the wrong location. But if you set out to earn good money doing work you understand, in a way that is good for you, that's a far more grounded and realistic path.

With that awareness, you can stop comparing yourself to others and start designing a business that actually fits *you*.

For me, business was never about maximising income. I didn't set out to start a business – I set out to start a life grounded in self-understanding, aligned with my personality and values. I was committed to working in a way that protected the balance of my energy because I wasn't going down the burnout path again. It was too painful the first time, as well as being expensive and impactful to me and the people I love.

It just so happened that small business suited what was important and good for me. It gave me a way to express my values in the world, to serve people in meaningful ways, and to design a life that allowed me to be present – mentally, emotionally, and physically – for the people I cared about most.

Of course, I didn't get it right from day one, and have had periods where the alignment has swayed. There have been plenty of stumbles and missteps. But through failure, reflection, and some good science, I figured out what was good and right for my nature, and I found a compass to guide me back to true north whenever I strayed.

Having walked that path myself, it felt deeply rewarding to help others navigate theirs. There's a term – *the wounded healer* – for those who can guide others because they've healed something within themselves. I suppose that's true for me. It creates an empathy that only experience can bring.

Perhaps that's why I've been particularly drawn to working with small business owners because their lives are fascinating – full of risk, reward, and decision after decision that either brings them closer to, or further from, the life they want. Not just practically, but emotionally – how they wish to live, feel, and show up for others.

I knew from the outset that my model of business had limitations regarding the financial returns it could provide. But that trade-off was a conscious one. It also gave me the space to explore different avenues of interest – what some might call side hustles, but for me were simply other sources of joy, creativity, and opportunity.

Even with a variety of interests, life never felt overwhelming (except for the time I took on that major renovation with the builder who went awry). Living and working in balance hasn't been luck – it was because I never forgot what I was in business for, and whenever I found myself off centre I corrected as quickly as I could. I was committed to doing business, and life, my way. I had made balance a non-negotiable. Every decision had to honour that value.

Balance, to me, is one of the greatest contributors to mental health. And mental health is everything. It's the cornerstone of being present, focused, and loving – in my work, in my family, and in my life. It's one of the gifts I endeavour to give everyone around me.

I recalibrate regularly. I observe my energy, what I'm saying yes to, what I'm saying no to, and how that all works for my nature. I'm observant of the activities of my mind and act so I can come back to balance again. The further off-track I go, the more awareness and courage it might take to come back. But the return path always starts with two questions: *what matters most? And what am I willing to do to protect that?*

This is compassion in action. Accepting the past, learning from it, attending to today with a sense of positivity for the future.

> Sometimes decisions are hard, but any decision that aligns your business and life with what is right and good for you is always worth it.

CHAPTER SUMMARY

The focus of this chapter is shaping your business environment to suit your nature – and then putting the right structure in place to help it hold its form. Sometimes putting this structure in place can feel like hard work, and something which actually goes against your nature. That's okay for a short period as long as you keep the bigger picture in mind.

If your business, and life, lacks the shape to do the basics well, you'll keep being drawn into problems, issues, and complaints. Therefore, we need to be clear on what's good and right for you, and willing to do the work to build the model that will match this. It can take time, but it's certainly worth it if you'd like a smooth and sustainable business journey.

Here's a summary of each section to help consolidate these insights:

- The starting point matters. Instead of asking 'what am I good at?', ask 'what's good for me?' Sometimes the environments where our skills take us don't actually serve our wellbeing, and that distinction changes everything.

- Recognise that everyone's nervous system has its own limits and tolerance for workload, pace, and people. Respecting yours is essential; ignoring it leads to stress and burnout.
- Growth without restraint creates chaos, while stagnation breeds frustration. The goal is measured growth – progress that fits your rhythm and offers some excitement, yet still keeps you grounded.
- Once you're clear on your ideal pace, place, and partners in business, take the reins. Define what you stand for and communicate it often until everyone around you understands it. Be the boss.
- With clarity comes alignment. Set expectations and create accountability so your business isn't shaped by outside influences or pulled off course.
- Resist the urge to chase every new idea. Consistently doing the 'boring stuff' well builds trust, steadiness, and mental space for clear thinking. Smooth really is good.
- Focus on the people who truly value what you offer – alignment with your right audience makes everything easier.
- Keep returning to your original motivation. Others will have opinions, but what matters most is staying anchored to why you're in business in the first place. Stay true to that motivation – and to doing business in a way that genuinely fits you.

In the next chapter we look at interacting with others. From my two decades of supporting small business owners, the most prevalent challenge and frustration among my clients is how to deal with other people.

Let's face it, dealing with others can be complex, confusing and at times frustrating. It can evoke all types of emotions, and at times bring out the worst in us. On the flipside, it can also be incredibly inspiring, encouraging, and rewarding. And ironically can also bring out the best in us.

So what is it that leads to frustration, and what leads to connection? How can we navigate our daily interactions such that we can be true to ourselves and also function in a way that reduces burnout risk?

Understanding this is gold for any small business owner, especially those with leadership or management responsibilities.

The way you interact and deal with others can make or break a small business, and is foundational to sustainability. There is no perfect science here, but there are plenty of insights and strategies that every small business owner can draw upon.

Before we take that next step, let's pause to reflect on a few questions from this chapter on alignment.

Reflective questions for the alignment: matching your business to you

Below are a set of reflective questions inspired by the key insights from this chapter. *Choose three that resonate most with you, and allow yourself a few minutes to explore your thoughts and feelings honestly.*

These reflections aren't just exercises; they're opportunities to uncover clarity, strengthen self-awareness, and take meaningful steps towards living and working in alignment with what truly matters to you.

1. Start with what works for you, not what you're good at

Consider how suitable your current business model is to your natural inclinations, personal preferences and what you value. In what way does it suit you?

In what way does it not suit you?

What changes could you make to increase alignment?

2. Your business model needs to match your nervous system

Is your business model working with you, or against you? Is it keeping you awake at night or agitating your nervous system?

Is your business vision in alignment with what feels right and sustainable for you?

If so, what do you need to keep an eye on so you can move towards this vision with ease and composure?

3. Measured growth

Do you feel you have tried to grow too fast, or too slow? Is it time to make some adjustments?

4. Be the boss

In what ways have you stepped back from actively leading your business or life? What might have caused that shift and how can you step back in?

Do the people around you have a clear sense of your business direction – and why it matters?

Are you making intentional decisions, or mostly reacting to what's urgent or loud?

5. Accountability and expectations create shape

Where is your business starting to feel loose?

What's one change, conversation or boundary that could help bring things back into shape?

6. Boring beats sexy

Is your business running smoothly?

Are you executing on time and budget?

If the answer is no, identify five basics which are not being completed as well as they could be in your business.

7. Value is personal

What do your most engaged clients/customers value about your service/product?

How can you use this knowledge to articulate your value in a way that resonates with your prospective clients?

8. Remember what you're in it for

Why did you first go into business?

Has your reason for being in business changed?

What could you do to bring your business into further alignment?

04

INTERACTION: DEALING WITH OTHERS

Give your plants what they need,
not what you need. In turn, they'll give you
what you need, not what they need.

The ecosystem is everything. Burnout risk can be significantly heightened, or reduced, according to who we have in our life and business, and how we deal with those people, and how they deal with us.

A calm mind can be easily unsettled by an uncomfortable interaction. One odd moment isn't usually a problem, but repeated friction, even small, can gradually leave us feeling tense or on edge.

In this chapter, we'll explore practical approaches for navigating interactions in a way that supports your wellbeing. The aim is to cultivate a culture and ecosystem that, on the whole, aligns with your nature and helps you operate with greater ease.

I have seen these approaches be extremely helpful for small business owners managing a team, interacting with clients, and engaging with other business owners. Equally, I have seen positive outcomes from using these principles at home and in other social and community environments.

While these principles have been proven to be helpful in relationships, it's important to be honest about something: some people are just not for you, and you're simply not for some people. And this is okay.

Sometimes two people sincerely try to make a relationship work. But regardless of the effort and intention, you have a way of getting on each other's nerves and just feel unsupported or unvalued. Neither person is really meaning for this to be the experience, but something just doesn't click.

Then in other cases, the opposite happens. You meet someone and hit it off straight away. It feels so aligned that it's impossible for it not to click. There's hardly any effort required. There's a remarkable comfort. A lightheartedness, humour, yet still a sense of sincerity, care, and compassion.

So why does it click with some and not with others? Well, I'm not sure and would need to do a lot more research before I would feel qualified to comment on this. But what I do know is if we look at nature, this attraction and repulsion isn't limited to humankind. The experienced vegetable gardener knows some types of plants grow better together than others. So even in nature, there is something that lends certain things to function better together, and others not so.

What we can learn from this is we don't need to force a relationship into a certain shape, because maybe it was never meant to be in that shape in the first place. Accepting this is helpful, and will certainly reduce the likelihood of contorting and shape shifting ourselves just to appease another.

> Without force and unrealistic expectations,
> we can go forth and interact with both those
> we click with and those we don't in a way that is
> healthy for us, and for them.

Maintaining a healthy perspective in your interactions is valuable. It helps you stay clear, avoid turning small issues into big ones, and engage with others in ways that reduce unnecessary stress. This matters more than it might seem. When you create a culture and environment free from excess tension, you strengthen your burnout-proof foundation.

In this chapter, we'll look at practical approaches that generally lead to better outcomes when dealing with others. Of course, when it comes to people, there are no guarantees – but these principles can greatly improve your chances of positive, balanced relationships, without feeling you need to become something you're not.

COMPASSION FIRST

I remember when I wasn't at my best – when I hit burnout, resigned from my job, and felt lifeless and without value.

Some people around me were compassionate. Others struggled. Those who struggled couldn't understand why I felt the way I did, and without that understanding, they found it difficult to empathise.

About a decade later, I attended a workshop where the group was discussing depression. Feeling brave, I shared parts of my burnout story, including how I had felt depressed. The teacher responded, 'If you didn't feel like that for three consecutive years, you don't know what depression is really like.'

While the comment may have been true, it left me feeling disregarded, and I found myself quietly withdrawing from the conversation. I do remember the impact that moment had. It left me with a lasting insight: a compassionate ear builds trust; a sharp tongue can dissolve it.

> Suffering is suffering, whether or not it meets a clinical definition, aligns with a diagnosis, compares as greater or lesser to another's experience, or makes sense to the intellect.

Experiences like this remind me how important it is to listen with patience, curiosity, and care. From that day, I made a personal commitment to listen more deeply. I know there have been many times when I could have been more compassionate. I haven't always got it right, but I believe my average has improved.

To offer a compassionate ear, it helps to be in a good headspace. Chapter One explored some ways to support this, such as finding a sustainable tempo for business and life. When my schedule is tight and my mind is full, it's harder to be at my best for others.

I've had some people suggest that being compassionate isn't their natural style or inclination. If I asked my 25-year-old self if

I was compassionate by nature, I probably would have said no as well. I might have said I was considerate, at least within my ability to tune in to what others needed. I would never intentionally want to make someone's life difficult or be the cause of pain.

I'm not alone in this. Over the years I've worked with hundreds, if not thousands, of people with all kinds of values hierarchies and personality orientations. I'm yet to meet anyone who genuinely desires to be the cause of difficulty or harm. Generally speaking, I've found people to be considerate and compassionate by nature, although this can sometimes be expressed in unusual or unexpected ways. It is only when someone feels pushed into a corner, fighting for their own survival physically or psychologically, that this can shift.

To deepen our ability to offer compassion and consideration, one thing I've learned is that if I only listen with my intellect, I miss what is really going on. I have to quiet my mind and listen not just to the words but to what sits beneath them. I try to sense what is being said and what is not being said. I listen for what matters to the person, what they care about, what they fear. I try to listen in a way that puts me in their shoes, rather than imagining how I would handle the situation they're in or difficulties they face.

I've found it helpful to genuinely believe people are doing the best they can. We are all working with a kind of Pandora's box of conditioning from our upbringing, our social environment, our values, personalities, likes, dislikes, and fears. These differences create the potential for misunderstanding or frustration. But when I accept people are doing their best, a quiet sense of compassion and consideration settles in. It brings more ease within me, and with it a greater ability to think clearly and broadly.

This approach seems to bypass the intellect. It gives me a better chance to stay compassionate even when things don't go my way. It reminds me that understanding *why* someone feels a certain way is often complex – and that needing to understand every detail can actually block connection. When I stay with compassion instead, the connection remains, and in time, deeper realisations come.

A few years ago, I had a client come in complaining about the attitude and performance of one of their staff members. They spent a few minutes talking about what the staff member wasn't doing and the generally negative attitude they brought into the environment. The staff member came across as being cocky and argumentative, and my client was finding this attitude infuriating.

I was empathetic with my client as they were clearly finding the whole situation upsetting. I made sure I expressed my empathy and reaffirmed that I appreciated suffering is not nice and is hard to deal with. With that warm expression of compassion, my client settled, and we had the mental space to work through the situation together.

I asked, 'Do you think your employee is happy working in your business?' My client said they didn't know. I shared a bit about my own experiences and what I've observed over the years – that people are often hardest to manage when they're unhappy.

The following week, my client met with the employee and asked a simple question: 'Are you happy here?' The motivation behind the question was to find out what it was like for the employee on a day-to-day basis, not in terms of productivity, but in terms of engagement and enjoyment. The employee said *no*. Through a genuine and caring conversation, it became clear that they didn't enjoy the type of work the business primarily delivered.

There wasn't much my client could change – that service was the core of the business. A few days later, the employee decided to resign, realising they weren't at their best and needed a change.

The separation was handled with mutual respect, allowing both to move forward with clarity and goodwill.

Sometimes an employee or client may not be in their best form. If you have it in your capacity, offer an ear of compassion. There may be significant changes required, such as the employee or client moving on. In other circumstances, a change in management structure may be the result, or a change in the way services are delivered.

Perhaps no change is needed at all, and a conversation is all that is needed.

> Whatever the situation or the results, it's possible to manage all aspects of business and life with compassion as the foundation.

What I've noticed is when something isn't really working for one person, it's often not working for the other either. Compassion is a great foundation to approach anything and everything, but as mentioned, we need to be in a good place within ourselves to be able to do this.

GIVE THEM WHAT THEY NEED, NOT WHAT YOU NEED

I once worked with a passionate and ambitious business owner who was about 20 years into his journey. Early in his career, he had made his mark offering bold ideas that reshaped how a major company completed projects. Free-thinking came naturally to him, and over time, he brought that same entrepreneurial spirit into his own bustling business.

During a round of annual performance appraisals he offered each employee any desired professional development course they were interested in. It was a very generous gesture and something he believed would be good for culture and empowering for his team. Following the offer he waited with anticipation to see what studies his people would like to pursue. Hours and days marched by with no responses.

He was frustrated. Of his 15 employees not one took him up on his offer. He couldn't understand why they weren't inspired to grab such an opportunity. His interpretation was that no one was grateful for the offer, nor motivated to develop themselves.

I explained that not everyone operates well with that sort of freedom. Some people need more structure to move forward confidently.

I shared a simple example: imagine coming home after a long day and being asked, 'What would you like for dinner?' He paused, wondering where this question was going, and then saw my angle. He said, 'Sometimes I'm too busy with other things and don't really want to make another decision.'

I replied: 'Even you, someone who likes to think laterally, differently and make up your own mind, can come to a place where too many options is limiting – not liberating. It may be easier for you to come home to one of two choices – for example, would you prefer lasagne or stir-fry?'

> Many employees thrive not with endless options but with clear pathways, with a defined number of choices.

To meet them where they're at, he could have:

1. Asked each person if they were interested in further professional development.
2. If so, offer two general options; for example, leadership skills or technical skills.

3. Presented two or three specific course suggestions within their chosen area.

By narrowing the choices, he would support his team in a way they could easily engage with. He would provide a platform that suited them. In turn, he creates the possibility for his team to engage in further development, which is something his business would benefit from. This approach may feel a bit cumbersome for him as this isn't the way he would generally like to complete such a process. But it would land much better for the nature of the people in his team.

I wouldn't be asking him to hand-feed his employees all the time, as we need to give room for people to show how they can step up under their own motivation. But sometimes we do need to create a rung for them to step on.

This principle applies far beyond training offers. Many employees feel stressed and uncertain when directions are too vague. Clear guidelines don't just boost productivity – they protect wellbeing and create a healthier, more effective culture.

> Leadership often isn't about offering what you would want – it's about offering what others need to succeed.

The specific needs of others are often different from your own, especially when we compare the nature of someone who decides to take on the challenge of small business compared to those who prefer employment.

Helping others be successful in a way that suits them makes life easier for you. To help with this it's important to truly comprehend the needs of others.

COMPREHENSION IS DIFFERENT FROM COMMUNICATION

It's a common human trait to struggle with deep listening. Often, we hear just enough to form a relatable story of our own – and then, without even realising it, we begin waiting impatiently for the other person to finish so we can turn the conversation back to ourselves.

I know this well. For many years, I did the same thing – more out of habit than intent – believing this was how conversations worked. These days, I'm more mindful of this tendency and make a conscious effort to listen more deeply and for longer.

True connection isn't just about talking or sharing your own experience – it's about genuinely feeling and understanding the other person. It's about taking the time to listen to their words, notice their energy, and tune in to what's behind what they're saying. It's about being fully present. That kind of listening means staying engaged – not just with the content of their story, but with how they're telling it. It means resisting the urge to steer the conversation towards yourself and staying with their experience just a little longer.

One practical way to do this is by staying on topic. If someone is talking about their child, focus on their child – don't pivot to a story about your own. That doesn't mean your experience isn't valuable; it just means that, in that moment, your presence and attention are the greatest gifts you can give. You can share your story later – once they've felt fully heard.

The same applies at work. If a colleague opens up about a challenge, resist the reflex to immediately respond with one of your own. Let their story breathe. Giving someone space to express themselves, without interruption or redirection, helps them feel validated and understood – and it deepens the connection between you.

Of course, old habits can creep in, especially when we're busy or distracted. So the next time you're heading into a conversation, ask yourself: am I truly listening, or just waiting for my turn to speak?

Try to stay with the other person's experience a little longer. You might feel uncomfortable. You may even feel bored at first. But with practice, you'll uncover a depth in others that you may have missed before.

> And in doing so, you'll find prioritising comprehension over communication leads to more meaningful, harmonious relationships.

For some, maintaining focus in conversation is difficult. If that's you, know that it's okay – this is a practice, not a performance. Be kind to yourself if you slip up. Harsh self-criticism only makes concentration harder. Remember, compassion first.

Sometimes it can help to be upfront. You might say, 'I just want you to know my mind is really distracted today, so I'm sorry if I jump in or interrupt.' That simple honesty can defuse tension and build trust.

And even if deep listening doesn't come naturally, I've seen people with highly distracted minds improve significantly, myself included. With patience and commitment, they've learned to hold their focus longer, interrupt less, and understand more deeply. They're not trying to be something they're not; they're simply letting go of an old habit of being unconsciously swept up by their mind's activity.

Seeking to comprehend is one of the most powerful foundations for effective communication. The more we comprehend, the less frustration we're likely to experience, which then positively affects not only what we say, but how we say it – in other words, our tone.

TONE TELLS THE STORY

'I don't just listen to words – I listen to the use of words, to the feeling behind the words, I listen to the tone. I listen to what isn't being said.' I remember sharing this with a client after a board meeting where something seemed off – the words were fine but the tone was not.

Some people speak harshly without even realising. Others use a harsh tone because they assume it doesn't matter. Others are simply tired and frustrated and fall into a harsh tone, which for them is out of character.

Some business owners use a harsh tone to assert authority. This approach is fast becoming a relic, as it's a shortcut to division, not collaborative leadership.

Whatever the cause, the effect is the same: a harsh tone leaves a mark. It shifts the atmosphere. It changes how people feel.

Tone creates culture.

So before you start planning a culture workshop, take a look at your tone – because if that's off, no amount of workshops will overcome the effect of repeated unsavoury tone. A poor tone is a culture killer.

As we deepen in patience and acceptance, tone naturally softens. And when it softens, people feel it. The words seem to ride on a cloud of ease and grace. Tension dissolves.

Tone tells the story. It reveals where someone's at within themselves and how they feel about the people around them.

> A softer tone is a signal: it says 'I see you, I value you, and I'm not here to overpower you.' That's the kind of tone worth building a culture on.

I recall being part of a business networking group. The culture was really good and had the potential to be outstanding – but there was one member who dragged the vibe down. It wasn't that they were trying to do this; in fact, they were well-meaning. But they were overly attached and unreasonably particular about how everything should be. As a result, they were easily frustrated and very unhappy. Having a different point of view is no problem, but the tone with which their opinion was delivered created a lot of division.

Given my sensitivity, I felt this deeply. This was compounded as I also love to see people make choices that put them in the right spot at the right time for their happiness.

Given this person's inner state of unhappiness and frustration, whenever they communicated, the tone hit everyone before the message of their words. Over time, it didn't matter what the actual suggestion or comment was – the tone led the charge and dragged everything down.

When this person decided to leave the group, there wasn't disappointment – just a solemn sigh of relief. I felt sad it didn't work out for them, but also happy, because they made a higher decision to change their environment. I'm hopeful this decision led to more happiness for them individually and for everyone around them.

> Tone shows us not only how someone is within themselves, but also how suitable their current environment, including their business model, is to their nature.

Interestingly, the tone used in our speech often reflects the tone of our thoughts. Therefore, making an effort to think less abrasively can directly assist speaking with a more positive and supportive tone. Thinking with less judgement and criticism will certainly help as well.

To become more aware of the effect of tone, observe how it changes your environment and quality of conversations and interactions. You may not be overly sensitive to this to begin with, but keep observing. Your ability to pick up these communication nuances can help you become more sensitive to the tone you use, and the effect it has on others.

ALWAYS CORRECTING CAN CREATE INSECURITY

A sense of security is a basic human need, and a lack of it can lead to a lot of discomfort within. Anxiety, panic attacks, and sleep difficulties are common outcomes when someone feels insecure.

Insecurity can develop in many ways: through traumatic experiences, growing up with a lack of physical or emotional safety, or continual criticism that leaves us feeling inadequate.

In the workplace, if the majority of communication is based on correcting another's work and behaviour, we're conditioning the person to believe they're always coming up short. Second-guessing every action for fear of inadequacy is mentally exhausting and emotionally overwhelming. A person feeling this way will seldom be able to operate at their best – we simply can't when our nervous system is in overdrive.

This disempowerment may lead them to give up: *if I can't do a good enough job, I'll just do what I can and let others fix it, because it won't be adequate anyway.* Some people will be able to work in this reduced way, while others will be unable to, and will look to leave the workplace altogether.

A sense of safety matters, and acknowledgement is essential. Taking a break from constant correction can change the world for another. Find a way to say 'well done, what you have done with this part of the project is amazing'.

Balance between acknowledging positive performance, effort, or attitude, along with an organised way to provide feedback and guidance, is much more likely to yield positive behavioural, relational, and performance outcomes.

Having an organised structure for providing feedback is worth considering. Doing so creates predictability in the environment, and from my experience, the majority of people who seek employment value predictability at a very high level. A lack of it is scary, leaving their nervous system elevated when it doesn't need to be.

No one likes to be ambushed, and unfortunately I have seen complete relationship breakdowns where feedback and criticism was delivered randomly and without due consideration to timing.

Just as it's nurturing to give yourself a break from continuous improvement for a while, having structure around feedback enables your people to get on with their job or life without feeling as though they're always needing to process criticism.

While feedback is important and can certainly help your team, keep in mind that success and progress will be influenced by the way it's delivered.

To apply some of the concepts we have already explored, there's a tempo, tone, and perspective that will influence such success.

Tempo is steady, tone is caring and kind, and perspective is one of comprehension and positive regard.

Too little feedback can lead to errors and wasted effort. Too much can feel like micromanagement, which stifles confidence, learning, and autonomy. Finding the right approach is crucial. Let others know the purpose behind your feedback: not to catch anyone out, but to support progress towards shared goals. Ask your team members how they would like to receive feedback. Remember comprehension before communication.

Sometimes the content of feedback can be uncomfortable to discuss.

> In these cases, letting the shared goals be the leader is an effective way to navigate difficult conversations.

For example, I was working with a professional adviser who occasionally needed to give their clients feedback they knew wouldn't be well received or would be dismissed. My client was a very capable technician, and a sensitive and quiet person by nature.

As a result, providing unfavourable feedback had the tendency to make the adviser feel a little nervous, and the tension was beginning to affect their confidence. To manage the emotional weight while still having the necessary conversations, we focused on reinforcing common goals first and then providing feedback that aligned with these, according to an agreed-on schedule.

In this particular case, the shared objective was helping the client run their business with more effective financial control and clear reporting for the owners.

Previously, when the adviser had offered suggestions, the client agreed in concept but then didn't make it a priority and was slow to take action. This time, my client began by clarifying higher-level common goals: to increase the consistency of financial performance. The benefit of this is the reduction of stress, ease in business, and enhanced saleability of the business in the future. With this context clearly established, the same advice was delivered again.

This time, the feedback landed. The client was more receptive because the message was now clearly tied to something they cared about. It wasn't just a critique saying the financial control could be tighter – it was positioned as an essential contribution to their own goals.

When feedback is delivered in this way, it helps create a culture of authentic alignment, rather than a sense of criticism, judgement or frustration. It helps the receiver more deeply connect with the value of the feedback for themselves, as well as seeing the value of it for the organisation, environment or culture they're in.

Use this approach and you'll increase the likelihood of building an environment that is progressive, stable, and deeply supportive, and feels that way too.

GAIN PERMISSION BEFORE GIVING ADVICE

There's something quietly unsettling about receiving unsolicited advice. Even when it's well-meaning, it can feel intrusive – like someone trying to take over the steering wheel of your life or business without asking if you'd like help driving.

For the person offering advice, it often comes from a good place – care, concern, or enthusiasm. But it also carries assumptions: that the other person wants to change, should change, or even sees things as a problem in the first place.

> Often people seek change in another not because it serves the other person's needs but because it serves their own.

When I first started my coaching business, I was full of excitement about what I thought could help others. That excitement, mixed with naivety, led me to offer advice far too quickly – and sometimes without asking if it was even wanted.

Looking back, I see now that even if someone could have done something differently (in my eyes), that didn't mean they wanted to – or that it would've actually been better for them. The person craving change wasn't always them. Sometimes it was me. I was projecting something I was interested in without checking if the other was interested themselves.

I learned to trust that my clients were inherently wise, thoughtful, and capable. My job wasn't to instruct based on my opinions, but to support the development of insight and clear decision making – to offer ideas and help them decide what was right for them.

And here's the beautiful twist: when I stopped needing to be the director of change, I felt more peaceful. Less pressure. More presence. I moved from being the 'expert adviser' to a genuine partner in life and business.

I have found there is a quiet yet powerful outcome when my focus is to ask people what they want to work on, and letting this guide our conversations, investigations, and new initiatives.

This approach of curiosity first, and resisting the temptation to forge forward with advice, shows composure and respect.

I was chatting with a small business owner the other day and he was sharing about the difficulty of managing cashflow given the seasonal nature of his business. We were talking in a public area after a business networking meeting. Another business coach turned up and introduced themselves. They tuned into the conversation, which was fine, but the next step was rather uncomfortable. They jumped in explaining to the small business owner he should increase his fees and let people go during the quieter times. On the surface these are fair considerations, but the advice wasn't requested and just forced upon the business owner.

I couldn't figure out if it was just enthusiasm or a marketing strategy of 'look how much I can help you and how much I know'. Regardless, the conversation became one-sided, the business owner went quiet, and within another sentence or two, we all found a reason to leave.

> The moral to the story is to stay interested in others and avoid giving advice unless it's asked for. If you really want to make a suggestion, first ask if the other person is interested in hearing it.

An interesting exercise I use with my clients is the 'Should Exercise'. I ask them to write the name of someone they interact with regularly – a business partner, employee, or client. Let's say their name is Charlie. Then we complete the sentence: 'Charlie should … '

If Charlie is an employee, the sentence might be: 'Charlie should be more focused at work and less distracted.' Or: 'Charlie should be more interactive with the team.'

This exercise reveals the expectations my client has for Charlie – the unspoken standards Charlie is failing to meet.

As a business owner, it's tempting to act on this list – to tell Charlie what needs improving. But doing so without context-setting dialogue can feel like an ambush. Charlie might feel blindsided, especially if they thought they were doing a good job.

So we shift from 'should' to 'could' – Charlie could be more focused with their work.

This change in language shifts our mindset from criticism to possibility. Now we're in a better frame of mind to say: 'Hey Charlie, I have a few ideas I'd like to run past you about workflow. Would you be open to a catch-up?'

Depending on the strength of the relationship, and Charlie's nature, they may still be a little nervous. But at least the topic of conversation has been clarified – sharing ideas about workflow – and Charlie has been invited to be involved. Charlie can say no – and that gives you useful insight into where they're at, perhaps prompting a deeper HR discussion. But most of the time, Charlie says yes.

From there, a more constructive conversation can take place. You might say: 'Some tasks are taking longer than we have budgeted. I'd like to see if there are some efficiencies we're missing or if we're not allocating time appropriately.' It becomes a conversation, based on comprehension first, as well as taking into account different perspectives. It's based on a shared goal – to develop more efficiency while respecting reasonable expectations – and an open dialogue grounded in curiosity and collaboration.

We're not dictating change; we're co-creating solutions. We believe Charlie has something valuable to contribute. You're still the boss and will ultimately have to make critical business decisions, but at least the opportunity to develop genuine understanding has been established.

Of course, managing others towards an organisational goal does mean offering feedback and guidance. But how we do this matters.

> Requesting permission before offering input might seem too slow for the busy and ambitious business owner. But the impact of unsolicited advice shouldn't be underestimated.

Its psychological effect is real. It can make people feel judged, misunderstood, or defensive. It often shuts down dialogue rather than opening it up.

But when we simply ask, 'Would you like a thought on that?' – we offer respect, not control. We become collaborators, not dictators. Most people welcome guidance. But how we deliver it makes all the difference – to the relationship and to the outcome.

BE WILLING TO LET GO

> How long do we hang on for when something isn't working?

It's a hard question to answer, and often the right answer is 'it depends'.

Different situations call for different levels of patience, but ultimately there needs to be a decision. For some people, letting go of something that isn't working is a remarkably difficult thing to do.

I worked with a gentleman who wasn't actually in small business when he came to me. He was a dedicated employee for a local firm. He was questioning if his chosen occupation was right for him. We analysed his nature and preferences, and then looked at how these were being supported or compromised in his work. What we found was that the industry probably wasn't ideal for him, although we could certainly find an approach to help it fit such that it could still work.

We uncovered the real challenge: the nature of his interactions with colleagues. The culture was relentlessly results-driven, and while he consistently hit his key performance indicators, many others were falling short. Sales meetings often spiralled into negativity, and he felt himself being pulled down by the weight of that atmosphere.

Even though his results were solid, he couldn't shake the sense that criticism was aimed at him. In reality, it wasn't – but when the air is thick with blame and frustration, it's almost impossible not to be affected by it.

We spoke about him setting up his own business. While the idea intrigued him, his loyalty was so strong that he could never make the step. In time, the environment started to hurt him.

His confidence dipped as he continued to be exposed to generalised criticism and negativity, yet he still stayed.

He was unwilling to let go of something that was clearly unhealthy for him, and this was pushing him to a point of emotional exhaustion and mental burnout.

Then Covid came along and he was no longer required to go into the office environment and started to work from home. His mental freshness started to return, as well as his emotional health. He found more energy for his work, and continued to kick goals – using only a fraction of the energy he had previously needed.

The difference was palpable.

After the Covid period, he started to go back into the office. The environment started to drain him again, and as a result he was able to confirm, without doubt, what he needed to change.

Within about six months he took the step to establish his own small business, where he could do business his way and develop a culture that was rich and nurturing for him. What he learnt was that culture is the foundation for his health, and therefore a culture that doesn't suit him is not good. It was a big deal for him to let go of his employment. He valued loyalty at the highest level and had great respect for his previous employer.

It was a moment of being stuck between a rock and a hard place, where he had to decide between what was going to be healthy and sustainable for him versus trying to uphold his value of loyalty.

When it came to prioritising his health and minimising burnout risk, he made the right choice. It was time to kill the chameleon and stop trying to adapt.

Letting go of a relationship can be hard; it can hurt. Sometimes you're the one letting go, sometimes it's another. It can make you think all kinds of weird things about yourself and other people. But, when we're honest with ourselves, we usually know what's working and what's not, and if we wish everyone to be happy, letting go can become the right action. In many cases, it's the most compassionate thing to do.

CHAPTER SUMMARY

Many people find it a little confusing at first – how could the way we deal with others possibly affect our risk of burnout?

To clarify: burnout risk can be magnified by the nature of the environment around us. And we directly influence that environment through how we interact with it – and especially with the people in it. In fact, one of the most powerful forces shaping our work environment is the people we work with, serve, and rely on.

Many small business owners bend and sway to try to accommodate others, whether employees or clients and customers. This sees the chameleon in full force. And often leads to frustration and exhaustion. Finding a respectful and compassionate way to interact with others, while staying true to yourself, is the major message of this chapter.

This understanding plays a major role in the sustainability of the structure you've built around you, and the vibrancy of the people within it. And those two things are deeply influential in determining whether you'll be able to go the distance in business and genuinely thrive with clarity and authenticity.

Let's recap the key points:

- Approach others with compassion. Without it, honesty can become harsh, shutting down communication and creating instability.
- Instead of giving people what *you* would want, focus on giving them what *they* need. This shift helps others thrive – and supports your own success too.

- Go beyond communication to true comprehension. When you focus on understanding, distractions fade and your presence strengthens. This changes relationships and environments alike.
- Remember that tone carries as much weight as words. Notice your tone, soften it where needed, and observe how people respond.
- Avoid the impulse to constantly correct. People need safety, encouragement, and the sense that they're doing well. Balanced, thoughtful feedback builds trust and calm.
- Gain permission before offering advice. It's a small step that reduces defensiveness and helps your message land.
- Know when to let go. Even with your best efforts, not every relationship or partnership will work. Holding on too long drains energy and increases mental load and burnout risk.
- Ultimately, how we deal with others shapes the culture and energy around us – in business and in life. This is a major contributor to ease and sustainability.

Next we look into the two final steps to creating a truly burnout-proof business and life. The first is finding a healthy way to move forward with what you've already discovered. After that, we look at the final step: recognising the value of acceptance.

But before that, let's pause to consider a few reflective questions to help you strengthen and personalise the insights from this chapter on interacting and dealing with others.

Reflective questions for the interaction: dealing with others

Below are a set of reflective questions inspired by the key insights from this chapter. *Choose three that resonate most with you, and allow yourself a few minutes to explore your thoughts and feelings honestly.*

These reflections aren't just exercises; they're opportunities to uncover clarity, strengthen self-awareness, and take meaningful steps towards living and working in alignment with what truly matters to you.

1. Compassion first

When was the last time someone truly listened to you with compassion? What impact did it have?

_____

_____

Do you tend to need to understand someone's struggle before you can feel compassion for them? How might you practise letting go of that need?

_____

_____

2. Give them what they need, not what you need

Do you tend to communicate with others the way you like to receive communication?

_____

If so, who around do you have most communication difficulties with? For that person, explore whether more detail and clearer guidelines, tighter check ins, or offering more scope would help. Test your theories with deeper listening.

___

3. Comprehension is different to communication

When was the last time you felt truly heard in a conversation? What happened?

___

How can you offer that same experience to someone else today?

___

4. Tone tells the story

Take a moment to reflect on when the tone in your voice goes from easy to harsh. Notice what leads to this and if there's a pattern.

___

Consider how tone influences the culture of your business, or family unit. Is it currently healthy or unhealthy? Could you enhance the tone used to further develop a respectful, supportive and positive environment?

5. Always correcting can create insecurity

Do you prefer to provide feedback and critique on the run or do you take time to work through improvement opportunities with others?

If you're providing feedback on the run, would bringing in more structure help with your delivery and how it's received?

Do you provide positive acknowledgment as a standalone communication? That is, not as a precursor to criticism?

6. Gain permission before giving advice

How often do you offer advice without checking whether it's welcome?

What might change if you paused to ask permission first?

7. Be willing to let go

Do you have any business or personal relationships that feel consistently stressful, strained, or combative – even when you put in effort? If so, is it time for a restructure?

05

PROGRESSION: MOVING FORWARD

A plant in the perfect spot still needs to convert sunlight into energy and transform that energy into growth. There is still work to do, even with perfect alignment.

Even when everything is aligned, and we're feeling balanced within, a certain amount of effort is still required. The amount of effort we're after is an appropriate amount such that we don't burn ourselves out.

If there's too much effort, that will throw us off balance, and then burnout becomes a risk again. If there's too little effort, business and life will get loose. This often leads to disorder and poor results, which turns into stress, and too much stress can also lead to burnout.

So the effort needs to be just the right amount, with just the right focus, such that we continue to work in a way that's right for us at a personal level, in a sustainable way.

To say putting all of this into practice is easy would be inaccurate. Small business, and life, has so many moving parts for this to be a simple process, but it is certainly possible to make positive steps of progress.

I have seen such progress many times over. But it's easy to slip back to old habits, and therefore regularly recalibrating focus to your highest priorities is important.

A busy person, with a busy mind, is the most vulnerable to straying off path. So stay clear, know what matters most, and move forward with balanced effort. Your future self will be deeply grateful.

In this chapter you'll find tips, ideas, and strategies on how to turn what you have learnt into real outcomes.

RELEASING VALUE

In the first meeting with all of my private clients I cover a very important topic: how to obtain value from the time and money they are putting into our work together. While it's tempting to get straight into other material, this is an important conversation if we're genuine about achieving positive results and real transformation.

I explain: 'To gain value from our work together, you need to turn up and give sincere thought and consideration to what we discuss. But what's even more important is your reflection and experimentation between our meetings.'

Yes, there's real value in the time we spend together. We broaden perspective, reset priorities, release frustration, renew respect for ourselves and others, and refine our commercial focus and direction. But that value can fade quickly if, the moment you walk out the door, there's no continued effort or reflection. For genuine change – moving from stress to clarity, from uncertainty to confidence – there needs to be an ongoing interest in the work we're doing.

Habits run deep. Without sustained attention and genuine desire, transformation simply doesn't take hold. To unlock lasting value, the spark must stay alive beyond the initial insight – nurtured by both thoughtful reflection and consistent action.

As an example, I caught up with one of the early readers of the manuscript of this book. From his reading, he came to realise that as an enthusiastic employer, he can be quick to give advice whenever it comes to mind. After reading the section on gaining permission before giving advice, he decided to take a slightly different approach.

When he next met with one of his key staff members, he set up the conversation a little differently. He said something along the lines of: 'I have an idea … do you mind if I run it past you?' The staff member open-heartedly and open-mindedly accepted the invitation, and they went into conversation.

His ideas and suggestions were well received, and the staff member seemed genuinely engaged in the conversation, and offered some of their ideas as well. While on the surface it seemed similar to previous conversations, it did carry a higher level of engagement.

Further to that, the business owner felt better about the way he handled the situation, which in turn enabled a more relaxed and peaceful state of mind.

If the business owner had simply read this book, and didn't reflect on his own habits, or consider what he could try a little differently, the value he would have realised from reading this book would have been less compared to what he actually experienced.

This example highlights that value often lies dormant until we act in mind, attitude, or practice. The application of ideas, insights, and realisations into real life is the very catalyst that releases value.

The goal of this book is to give you the platform to make real and beneficial change in your life, business and beyond. To experience this, you can't treat this like a gardening book and then never go out into the garden.

This is a book about life, us, people and its intersection with business.

The value in this book is somewhat dormant until you energise it with activity and attitude. The reflective questions at the end of each chapter can help with this, as can the sentences you have highlighted during your reading.

> Water your newfound seeds of wisdom with sensible yet meaningful new activity.

As you do this, be sure to respect where you are, and your current capacity, and measure each step with compassion and genuine self-consideration.

MEASURE YOUR STEP

'Just open the curtain and make the bed.'

That was my inner dialogue during recovery from burnout, all those years ago. Even though I had a clear vision of what I wanted – to live and work in a way that felt just right for my nature – I was completely depleted. I had almost no energy. I simply couldn't do much.

So getting out of bed, making it, and opening the curtain had to count as success. Any other perception felt unkind and unfair. I was doing my best, even if it didn't look like much. In that state, a positive attitude wasn't just helpful, it was essential. Any form of personal criticism had no place in my mind.

A week or so later, the next step was to walk around the block once a day. Then I layered in more: make the bed, have a shower, walk to the local park, watch the animals, and walk home again.

A month or so later, I could manage a regular day – still with minimal responsibilities – but with greater balance. After about six months, my capacity returned. I could once again function well, without falling out of alignment.

I share this to encourage you to be kind, be fair, and be realistic when thinking about the next steps you want to take. If your system is already stretched or fatigued, micro-steps may be the wisest choice. Slow and steady is not only fine, it's often necessary.

> You might even find yourself going two steps forward, one step back. That's okay. What matters is the overall direction, not perfection.

Maybe you're in a place of strength right now. If so, you might have the energy to try bolder ideas or take on bigger changes. Whatever your starting point, the ideal approach is the one that honours your current capacity.

And always remember: progress is not a universal standard. It's deeply personal. What's meaningful progress for one person may mean little to another. For some, it's practical – realigning ideal clients or adjusting your weekly pace. For others, it's philosophical – shifting priorities or reshaping self-perception.

Whatever your direction, trust your pace. Respect your capacity.

Progress is not about speed or comparison – it's about alignment. Take the next right step for you, even if it feels small.

> Small steps taken with awareness and intention can lead to the most powerful change.

Honour your process, and the path will keep revealing itself, one manageable step at a time.

LEVEL UP

Every now and then I see someone who is in the zone. Work is aligned to what suits them and they're flying. Then something happens. Somebody is unhappy at home, sales come down, a key employee decides to leave, or a business partner starts to show irritation.

In these cases, a significant issue has arisen and requires attention. Many clients say to me in these circumstances, 'I don't have time to deal with this right now.' In many cases they're right; they have so much else to attend to. The new matter feels more like a distraction than something they would really like to deal with. But the reality is, some matters can't be ignored.

In these situations, it's time to level up.

We don't need to drop everything to do so. It's simply a process of asking 'what could I do that would bring a better attitude, energy or outcome to … ' – whatever it is that needs attention.

I remember speaking with a successful business owner, who had experienced a lot of business growth. He had already levelled up with his desire to grow the business; however, he had levelled down his respect for his own needs for good mental and physical health. He had become socially isolated, disconnected from his family, and unable to switch off from thinking about business growth.

For some reason he believed business success would sort out everything else in his life, but the reality was everything else started to unravel. When we caught up, it had been days since he had properly spoken with his wife – whom he adored.

He had levelled down in looking after his personal welfare, and as a result, he was more irritable and reactive.

In his words, he was 'grumpy and not very nice to be around'. I asked if this is what he wanted. This may sound like an irrational question, but keep in mind I don't assume I know what is important to someone else, so I offer respect by checking before moving forward.

He said no; he didn't like being grumpy. We then agreed to explore options to bring about a better balance and, in turn, healthier relationships. Accordingly, we investigated ways he could level up the way he was around the people he cared about.

We identified what was draining his energy, so we could make some small changes which could lead to big results. In this case, it required a multi-pronged approach: adjusting work office layouts, bringing in specific organisational support, and enhanced reporting and accountability throughout the teams.

None of this could be executed if the desire to level up wasn't strong enough. In this case, it was, and he was willing to make changes in both his personal and business domains to improve the areas that were floundering.

Levelling up can take effort and energy you don't think you have. However, an honest appraisal of the likely outcome if we don't level up is important. For example, if sales are inadequate and you don't have the energy to level up in this regard, accept that business is unlikely to grow, and in the worst-case scenario you may go into liquidation.

Levelling up doesn't mean you start doing a whole bunch of activity you're not suited to, but it does mean you're willing to be responsible for results. So in the case of sales, you may engage someone to help with sales, meaning you still take overall responsibility; you're just not doing all of the activity yourself.

Areas where small business owners often need to level up are:

- financial control
- sales and marketing
- product and service development
- management of client suitability
- stress management and managing burnout risk
- strategic planning
- team development
- overall capacity management.

It can be a long list, so we need to be organised in our approach; otherwise, we go into overwhelm and can go back to burnout risk.

Identify what needs extra attention and decide how important it is. Then explore different ways the outcome could be achieved, all while accepting it's a work in progress.

Many business owners attempt to use discipline to drive these areas, but often wear themselves out in the process. I'd suggest reframing discipline and engaging freedom of choice instead.

REFRAME DISCIPLINE, ENGAGE CHOICE AND ACCEPTANCE

I have seldom met a small business owner who enjoys feeling obliged to do things in a certain way. In fact, most are slightly or significantly rebellious, and that's why they ended up in business ownership in the first place.

> Society tells us we need to be disciplined to achieve our goals.

Fair enough, there is evidence that high levels of discipline can enable someone to achieve, but this approach doesn't necessarily suit the rebellious.

I had a client who said he was sick of creating new goals. I asked why. His response was interesting. He said, 'I pursue my goal for a while and then for some reason I start to lose focus and have difficulty maintaining the discipline.' I shared that this isn't uncommon. What he said next was insightful: 'When that happens I feel terribly guilty as I have let myself down again.'

He was a free thinker and naturally curious. And he was tired of trying to 'do the right thing', on repeat, and in time failing, also on repeat. The idea that a lack of discipline was what blocked his progress had tortured him for more than a decade. The truth is he was a genuine man with strong family values, deeply loyal, and very good at his craft.

We had to find an alternative way for him to enjoy business that didn't feel so heavy. An approach free from obligation, resistance, and fear. One with more ease and joy. Less personal toll. One that still sees results but without the underlying 'no pain no gain' shackle.

This alternative approach would offer sustainability, longevity, and wouldn't make him puff and pant all the way to the finish line. It would provide achievement with more balance, and a sense of deep freedom and choice.

With this goal in mind, I asked him to write down at least five things he thought he should do in business. I asked him to do the same for his health and personal life. It wasn't hard for him to come up with five in each category. This is just like the 'should exercise' explained in the previous chapter but now applied to ourselves.

I then asked how he felt about each of these items. His response was aligned to our earlier discussion – they were all good ideas, yet he felt inadequate as he hadn't progressed them already. He felt like he had failed and should have done better, and as a result was inferior to others who he thought would achieve these things easily.

I assured him everyone had their challenges and to let go of comparison. I then asked him to accept his feelings of inadequacy, guilt, and any other emotions he was experiencing. I reminded him that we start with compassion, and that creates the space for clarity to be revealed.

The next step was to reframe his conditioned attitude towards goals and progress.

I asked him to rewrite each sentence, and instead of writing 'I should … ', to start each sentence with 'I could … '. So instead of, 'I should be more regular with my marketing activity', it now read, 'I could be more regular with my marketing activity.'

I then asked, 'So would you like to be more regular with your marketing activity?'

He said he would.

I said, 'Great. But let's be clear. You're under no obligation to do this. You're fumbling along with marketing at this stage, and it's going okay. However, you *can* make a different choice, not because you have to, not because anyone else is telling you to, but because there is some wisdom within you which you'd like to honour.'

He understood this difference and felt the shift. He felt comfortable. He felt empowered. He felt relaxed yet motivated. And before long, he was more regular with his marketing activity.

We worked through his other should and now could statements and clarified what was of interest for him to work on, and what was either to leave behind permanently or review at a later date.

A few years on, and this client is doing amazing. He occasionally goes back to his old obligatory way of thinking, but most of the time he knows he's making decisions with freedom. If something doesn't work out, he has more capacity to reflect without personal judgement, and explore new and more sustainable approaches.

Forced discipline is a thing of the past, yet progress is happening every day. And this progress is riding on choice, options, possibility and acceptance. Advancements in his business happen without unnecessary mental toil, and will continue to do so. His future will be better for this approach. He will see business success without exhausting his mind, such that he can engage with his family, friends, and other interests with energy and connection.

Progress will happen. Balance will exist. Burnout will not.

GOAL TO STRATEGY

'I don't want to do that anymore.'

These were the words of my client who recognised she really didn't want to offer a particular service anymore, which happened to provide approximately 25% of her annual revenue.

Interestingly, this desire wasn't new. It had roamed around in my client's mind for more than two years. Sometimes with more assertiveness, sometimes less, yet always there.

When wisdom like this is ignored for too long, perhaps because the desire to change is lacking or the suffering isn't enough, it still chips away at the gloss of our vibrancy. A small weight begins to form, which initially may go unnoticed, but over time can become heavy. This is what doing business as the chameleon feels like.

Serving this client segment was tiring for my client, and was unsustainable. If it was left much longer it would cause stress, anxiety, and general disengagement to a level which may have resulted in unfavourable knee-jerk decisions.

Our first step was to conduct a genuine consideration of options. This was important as sometimes we can feel stuck in a situation, and such a feeling stops us from being able to see alternative choices and opportunities. Before long, we had clarified her preference – to continue on with the business yet rationalise the client base such that it suited her.

This brought her desire into a clear goal – seen as an option, not an obligation. It was something she could act on if she wanted to. The idea was held lightly, joyfully, and with curiosity. Even a sprinkle of excitement.

We could then see the goal from a much higher perspective – not to just get rid of something (undesirable client group), but to proactively design exactly what her business did, and for whom, such that it had remarkable alignment to what was right for her, in this chapter of her business and life.

She could see this wasn't simply a business decision. This was much bigger than that. It was a chance to be the artist, and design and build exactly what would be good and right for her, for now and the years ahead.

Yet there was fear. What would happen 'if I lost a third of my revenue?'

This is where strategy comes in.

The development and execution of strategy is what makes goals happen.

The reason this change hadn't already happened came down to two things: the absence of conviction and no clear strategy for how to make it happen.

Without strategy, it's difficult to be proactive. We become overwhelmed by the noise of existing commitments and stay stuck in a loop until the discomfort grows so intense that it forces us to change – often through problems rather than choice.

A well-defined strategy prevents this. It creates a pathway from your current situation, which may no longer fit, towards one that's better aligned and sustainable.

In my client's case, the strategy focused on income replacement – expanding marketing into a new sector while gradually reducing the availability of services to be phased out. The plan would unfold over about six months, maybe a little more or less, but the direction was clear: we knew where we were heading, why, and how.

That clarity created excitement – and excitement fuels motivation. Progress then comes not from sheer discipline or over-exertion, but from a natural pull towards what works, supported by a clear sequence of steps.

In this case, it didn't take six months; the changes started to take shape almost straight away. Clarity and conviction lead the charge, and strategy ends up just being the practical steps to take.

> Strategy, built on clarity, is what transforms goals into reality. It's a critical foundation for thriving.

To convert our plans into reality, how we use time becomes the transformational catalyst.

EFFECTIVE TIME UTILISATION

So many things to do, so little time. This is the great crush of many small business owners, juggling demands and desires, in business as well as at home. We simply cannot be everywhere at once. Thinking we need to be is a very heavy burden.

How we utilise our time determines the effectiveness of our movement towards future goals, as well as affecting the quality of our sanity today.

I recall working with a brilliant businesswoman. She had experienced considerable growth, and had put a really good team around her. There was a rather long client list, which had been well served over the years. Through commitment and passion she turned up with vigour, week in, week out, year in, year out.

Then, after a decade, exhaustion started to kick in. And with exhaustion our minds start to play games – the dominant thought was *is this even worth it?* In this case, it certainly was worth it commercially, but the psychological demand, emotional drain, and loss of energy made it genuinely questionable.

I proposed a different way to think, and with that a different way to utilise time. Instead of being primarily focused on responding to the demands of business, we would be on the front foot with time management.

To do this, we first took a step back and asked what the vision was, and if it had changed from when the business started. Interestingly, it hadn't changed much at all.

However, what we noticed was a considerable change from the early days – the volume of client and employee demand on my client meant she was unable to lead with clarity as she had no time for reflection, refocusing, and enquiry. She was so consumed day to day, she was unable to see the bigger picture.

These 'higher level' activities – reflecting, refocusing, and enquiry – are sometimes referred to as 'working on the business'.

These are the activities that require proactivity and enable a business to function, with controlled shape, into the future. They include strategic planning, financial control and forecasting, marketing and networking, personal and professional development, research and design, and general business reflecting and envisaging.

Many of these activities were highly engaging and energising for my client, and they also allowed her to bring tremendous value to the business. However, engagement with these activities can often be sidelined when we are busy just trying to keep up with everyday demands. My client had disengaged with being on top of the business because she was so busy *in* it.

It would have been commercial suicide to remove her from all the client-servicing commitments overnight, although we did need a new game plan, a new strategy.

The goal was clear – to rebalance the usage of time. We knew the business needed the higher level thinking – 'working on the business' – as well as continued capability to deliver services and perform essential administrative functions.

Our job was to use time in a way that kept everything proactive rather than reactive. It was a big task, with plenty of change to navigate. This included refining internal processes and tightening accountability, which led to a couple of disruptive employees choosing to move on.

There was also an honest appraisal of client suitability, resulting in some clients leaving and new, better-aligned ones coming on board. Additional support was built into key management functions as well. Together, these changes led to more effective use of time overall, giving my client greater balance and a stronger grasp of her business.

As we move forward, this will reduce the likelihood that certain areas fall short, but when they do due to market changes or unexpected influences, there's a greater chance we'll be able to respond quickly with clarity, confidence, and a deeper understanding of the dynamics of the business.

These changes also delivered a very important outcome – my client went from being the chameleon, shape shifting to appease endless needs, to regaining control of what she did and how she did it. This empowerment enabled her to align her natural inclinations – big-picture thinking, creative problem-solving, and developing others – with her daily activities.

When realignment like this is achieved it's a game changer.

Importantly, the benefits of time utilisation to create balance and thereby reduce burnout risk don't just apply in business; they apply in all domains of life.

If you're not big on scheduling – and I'm certainly not – it's still worth recognising that how you use your time directly determines your results. These results reflect how time has been invested in the past. When that investment is off balance, the effects are obvious.

In the example above, the lack of higher-level thinking and constant demands from clients and staff created a serious imbalance. We didn't need to analyse it – the results, the environment, and the overall experience told the story. Results always mirror how time has been used in the past. As you've read through this book, you've probably had moments where ideas sparked – things you'd like to act on. But unless you deliberately make space for them, they'll stay as ideas. This isn't about discipline; it's about choice.

Time is one of your most valuable assets. If you feel like it's running you, pause and review how you're spending it. Look for balance across the areas that matter most.

If an activity consistently demands more time than you can give, find a more efficient way to handle it – perhaps by simplifying, systemising, or seeking help.

> The key lesson is not to chase time, but to stay ahead of it. Observe how you're using it, ensure it aligns with what's right and sustainable for you, and let it reflect your natural rhythm and the full spectrum of what matters to you in both business and life.

While the future cannot be guaranteed, what we do with our time today sows seeds of possibility for the future, which brings us to the next aspect of moving forward – the void between action and outcome – the lag effect.

THE LAG EFFECT

After working with so many small business owners over the years, I have come to believe the way a person uses their time, as explained above, along with their attitude provides a looking glass into what their future will look like.

I don't just mean having a positive attitude; it's far deeper than this. For example, clients who tend to go the distance with the least burnout risk have developed a certain attitude when something hasn't worked out. They reflect and learn. They don't blame; they take responsibility. They're willing to make new decisions.

They view any setbacks as opportunities to clarify what they're doing, why they're doing it, and what their future vision is. They clarify what the big objective is, and everything else falls into line under that.

Recalibration is regular, and with it, they bring a clear mind and confident focus. This creates balanced activity, ensuring they do the work which will provide the platform for future growth, along with what needs to be happening today to deliver products and services to their market.

Time utilisation is top of mind, along with a particular attitude.

This attitude balances the willingness to develop clarity for the future along with the backbone to execute what needs to be done today. There's no uncontrollable excitement or despair, just composure in action.

Seldom does this approach lead to something amazing today. But what it does do is lay the foundation for the future – and there is a certain amount of faith and belief that this effort today will lead to something.

Some people struggle with this last part. Their vision isn't strong enough to be able to stomach the lag between the effort today and the possible outcome in the future. When this happens, we need to go deeper with the development of vision, not just based on dreams but also the reality of needs in the marketplace. After all, there is no point being patient in business if what you're offering has no demand.

With a clear product or service offering, as well as a clearly defined need in the marketplace, one can find confidence in vision, take action, and then allow some time to see the effect of this action.

Let the lag effect play out for a little while. Then assess whether the efforts are building to what you had imagined. If not, make adjustments and watch again.

> It can take experience to figure out how much patience is appropriate. Without patience, there is just haste.

If we're always changing and not allowing the lag effect to show the outcomes of our efforts, we go back to being in an environment with serious burnout risk.

The lag effect is your friend. It's helping you take a moment to check your understanding, to fully comprehend the situation, and to develop composure of thought, which in turn will shape your action.

One area in business where the lag effect needs to be considered earnestly is succession planning, where you start to consider what actions, systems, and structures are needed for your ultimate exit from business.

SUCCESSION PLANNING – START EARLY

I see many smart businesspeople leave succession planning too late. It takes time to properly pull together the sale of a business, whether that's to an external buyer or to someone within the business. On average, I would say it takes around three years to do it well, and often a lot longer.

The transaction itself can be quick, but the value a business owner gets from the sale depends entirely on the quality and structure of the business. And getting that right is what takes time, energy, and deliberate focus.

I had a gentleman start with me a while back – sharp operator, but beaten down after about 23 years in business. He had a team of a dozen, but no top-end management support. When we first started working together, he was pretty close to quitting.

Initially, we found some strategies to reduce the pressure (many of these strategies have been shared earlier in this book). This gave him some breathing space and helped him steady the ship amidst all the daily challenges his small business was throwing at him.

Within a few months, he was lighter – clearer about where he was heading and what truly suited him. The fog had lifted, and with it came a renewed sense of purpose. It was time to ease the business's reliance on him and shape it into something that could stand strong on its own – a genuine and attractive opportunity for a future buyer.

To help execute the plan, we brought on an operations manager – it wasn't in a full-time capacity as the business couldn't afford that, so it was someone who could still be income-generating for a portion of the week. It made a massive difference. My client reclaimed some of his time and headspace, which allowed him to focus on business strategy and development instead of being stuck in the daily grind.

Fast-forward a couple of years – he had a stronger management structure, stronger financials, and even more business clarity. The market noticed this difference. Before he even went to the market to sell, offers started coming in from interested parties.

He went into negotiation with one of the potential buyers. Before long, a deal had been struck, and a favourable deal at that. This outcome was a direct result of a decision he made a couple of years earlier: to prepare the business for succession. He had completed the foundational work, the sale went through smoothly, and largely on his terms.

Pulling this together required energy. He came in tired, but we found some breathing space, developed a new vision that wasn't just about getting through the week. This created some new energy, and then the plan was executed.

Business owners who are 10, 15 or 20 years into business face serious burnout risk. They don't always close their doors like those who burn out early, but it can be a tough grind to the finish line. And the pain of this is exacerbated when they have no clear vision for succession or exit.

> Succession planning isn't just about exit – it's about setting up your business to run well, with reduced toll on you, whether you sell it or not.

Start this planning before you're tired. Start early. Develop a game plan. Execute it steadily, thinking at least three to five years ahead, and preferably longer.

Doing so is good for your business and good for you.

CHAPTERS HAPPEN

At the time of writing, I'm 52 years old.

I can't swim, run, or surf like I could a decade ago – and that's not a complaint, just an observation. I also find noisy environments more overwhelming, and bouncing back from a big day takes more time than it used to.

Business has shifted, too. I'm no longer chasing as much as I used to, nor am I juggling as many hats as I once did. There was a time when that pace felt exciting. But it's not where I'm at now.

These days, my work is more focused. My services are more niche. I do a lot less of what drains me – the networking, the corporate workshops, the extra promotions, the constant tweaking of systems. That stuff helped the business get off the ground. But it's not what fuels me now. It's not where I do my best work.

So does that mean I've lost my edge? Or am I just playing a different game?

Business owners often pride themselves on being resilient and relentless – and rightly so, because sometimes that's what it takes to survive. But what survival looks like changes over time.

The early chapter in your journey might be about proving yourself. The next chapter might be about preserving yourself. It becomes about tempo – knowing your rhythm, your energy, and where you add the most value. Letting go of being a chameleon and trying to be all things to all people. It's about choosing where to place your effort so you don't drain yourself and can function with flow and energy.

Chapters happen. We're not meant to operate the same way at 25, 45, and 65. The trick is noticing when you're coming into a new chapter – and giving yourself permission to adjust accordingly. As you move from one chapter to the next, explore how you'd like to do it differently and what you'd like to keep the same.

It's a privilege to be able to move into a new chapter on your terms. Many people don't have that opportunity.

CHAPTER SUMMARY

Once we have a base of clear understanding and an enticing opportunity, the challenge isn't believing what's possible – it's making space to let it become part of our lives. A full cup can't accept more water. A full mind can't entertain a new idea. And a full schedule leaves no room for evolution.

As we close this chapter, here are the key ideas to carry forward – practical reminders for turning insight into meaningful action:

- To unlock the value of any idea that resonated with you, breathe life into it. Small experiments and subtle attitude shifts can spark meaningful change. Be open to trying something that spoke to you from this book, even if it's just a gentle first step.
- Be fair and compassionate with yourself. You may not have endless energy or capacity right now, and that's okay. Micro steps still count – they create movement and momentum in the right direction.
- Ask yourself: *where might it help to level up?* Most business owners already know where things feel a little off. Write those areas down, and without judgement, explore small, manageable actions that could make a positive difference.

- This process isn't about obligation or pressure. It's about choice and opportunity. Set your own goals and surround yourself with the right people who can help you move forward. Support and collaboration often make the load lighter.
- Remember that goals and strategies are not the same thing. Goals define *what you want*; strategy shows *how to get there*. Give your goals a pathway – break them down into clear, achievable steps that feel realistic and grounded.
- Use your time wisely to work through these steps while managing your existing commitments. Be realistic with your timeframes. Progress doesn't need to be dramatic; steady, consistent effort layered over time builds powerful results.
- Change takes time. There's often a lag between action and outcome – sometimes weeks, sometimes months, occasionally years. Accept that progress can be slower than desired, but will happen with steady application of effort.
- Keep an eye on the long view. For business owners, the future can arrive quickly. Thinking early about how you'll eventually transition or exit allows you to shape that change with intention – often making a significant difference to both peace of mind and financial outcomes.
- And finally, remember that life and business unfold in chapters. Anticipate change and welcome it when it comes. Each chapter adds a unique layer to your story, and part of thriving is knowing when to close one and step into the next with curiosity and confidence.

In the next chapter, we'll focus on the foundation that allows everything else to fall into place, and the key to building a life and business that truly supports you, starting from where you are today.

But before we take that next step, let's pause to consider a few reflective questions to help you strengthen and personalise the insights from this chapter on moving forward.

Reflective questions for the progression: moving forward

Below are a set of reflective questions inspired by the key insights from this chapter. *Choose three that resonate most with you, and allow yourself a few minutes to explore your thoughts and feelings honestly.*

These reflections aren't just exercises; they're opportunities to uncover clarity, strengthen self-awareness, and take meaningful steps towards living and working in alignment with what truly matters to you.

1. Releasing value

On your way through this book, which ideas, stories, and reflective activities resonated the strongest for you?

_____

_____

Were they fleeting moments of insight, or have they stayed with you?

_____

_____

If any have stayed, pick one and consider what you could do to test out these insights in everyday business and life.

_____

_____

2. Measure your step

What's one small step you could take this week that feels helpful to your business, life or you?

_____
_____
_____

Are there any outdated expectations or internal pressures you could let go of to better honour your actual capacity right now?

_____
_____
_____

3. Level up

Identify areas in your business that need attention. Prioritise them, then ask, 'On a scale of 1 to 10, how much effort am I putting into this?' If you rate it a 5, ask, 'What could I do to raise it to a 7?' Make it achievable.

_____
_____
_____

Do you need to level up in areas which go against your natural inclinations and strengths? If so, what additional support could you engage?

_____
_____
_____

4. Reframe discipline, engage choice and acceptance

For activities or goals you would like to progress, do you feel obliged to do this, or inadequate as you haven't already?

_____
_____
_____

Can you change the way you think of these activities such that you're not acting under obligation, but indeed acting with choice and freedom?

_____
_____

5. Goal to strategy

List three activities or goals you would like to progress.

_____
_____
_____

Design a strategy to help bring these to life, which feels good and seems achievable for you.

_____
_____
_____
_____
_____

Would it help to have someone else to work with on the design or execution of your strategy(ies)? If so, who would this be?

6. Time utilisation

Do you feel like you run your schedule?

What activities are undervalued or under-supported in your business, or life?

How could you utilise time more effectively?

7. Lag effect

On a scale of 1 to 10, with 10 being the strongest, how comfortable and confident are you in your vision coming to fruition based on your current attitude and activity?

If your score is low, then do you need to adjust your vision, activity, or self-belief?

8. Succession planning – start early

Do you have a vision to sell your business in the future?

If so, who would the likely buyer(s) be, and what do you believe your business is worth? Would you like to enhance its capital value?

Have you developed a plan for what will happen to your business in the case you're unable to run it due to illness, injury, or death?

9. Chapters happen

What are some signs – physical, emotional, or mental – that a new chapter might be calling you?

Who or what do you need to let go of to make room for the next chapter?

_____

_____

_____

_____

Who or what do you need to bring in to transition into the next chapter?

_____

_____

_____

_____

06
ACCEPTANCE: HERE WE ARE

Such a simple phrase – 'here we are' – yet so full of truth and wisdom.

Here we are: the past behind us, ready for reflection but unchangeable. The future ahead, open to imagination, but not yet here – and perhaps it never will be.

This is the nature of being human.

We hold onto the past – in thought, emotion, and even in the body – and we carry an incredible ability to imagine what might lie ahead. Sometimes memory and imagination are our friends. Other times, they're stubborn, unwelcome guests.

That moment, years ago, when I woke up barely able to get out of bed, was one of the hardest in my life. But in hindsight, it was also one of the most transformative. It stopped me in my tracks and whispered: 'Here you are.'

It wasn't cruel. It simply revealed what years of repeated behaviours, unchallenged thoughts, and unconscious choices had built.

If anyone saw the train wreck coming, they kept it to themselves – which might have been for the best. My youthful energy and quiet arrogance would likely have deflected any warning. After all, I believed I was doing exactly what society had promised would lead to success, happiness, peace, and joy.

And then – in one mysterious stroke – I was shown the path to those very things.

The path didn't look anything like what I'd been taught.

When I surrendered, when I stopped pushing and striving … there it was: peace. Joy. Connection. No more achievements needed. No more time or milestones required.

That peace never left. It's always here – right here, right now.

Everything else is noise. Not bad noise, but loud enough to distract us from what's quietly, endlessly present: the silence, peace, and ease that is us.

So much of our striving – for success, for self-worth, for love or approval – is a well-meaning detour from the deep stillness within. I didn't find that stillness by design. I found it through exhaustion, by climbing the wrong ladder.

Or perhaps it wasn't the wrong ladder at all – it delivered me somewhere profound.

That moment became the foundation for my work, my business, my life.

Even as I came to know the deeper nature of who we are, I still felt a yearning:

- To live.
- To explore.
- To provide for my family.
- To create.
- To serve.

I didn't want to retreat to a garden and stay there forever. The garden had been a teacher – patient, grounding, and wise – but there was more to do. I could feel a quiet call to support others, especially those who, like I once did, risk losing their way: overdoing it, underdoing it, doing what doesn't fit, or simply losing sight of what matters most.

There was a gentle but persistent urging to help others build a way of doing business – and living – that feels genuinely good and right for them. And to do that, we must begin by accepting our nature and honouring where we are.

And where we are is here. Here we are. Here you are. And it's only from here that anything real can begin.

I know I've laid some paradoxes at your feet:

- Peace is within you now. And yet, build a business with a future vision.
- Be content. And discontent enough to refine, grow, and stretch.
- Be patient with life. And impatient enough to live it fully.
- Be kind to yourself. And still get up and give it another go.

These paradoxes aren't puzzles to solve with the mind – they're truths to embrace with the soul. In time, they won't feel contradictory. You'll know both can be true, even when they seem to pull in opposite directions.

It becomes a matter of judgement. Of sensing. Of knowing which lever to pull, and when, and how much.

And perhaps, that's one of the keys to becoming burnout-proof.

Learning how to move between effort and ease. Knowing when to act and when to rest. Approaching business – and life – as both science and art.

Because business isn't just a model, it's an expression.

It has design, structure, beauty.

It mirrors your focus, and when your focus is on authentically embracing and respecting yourself, your business feels natural, aligned, and true.

No more taking on an identity just to survive – it's time to thrive.

It's an opportunity to express your nature into the world, in a way that is good and right for you.

Stay true to that. Be clear. Trust yourself.

Thrive by being you.

No more chameleon.

A NOTE FROM THE AUTHOR

It's wonderful that you've arrived at this point. You've taken the time to explore how to live and work with deeper alignment – and that alone speaks volumes about your commitment to yourself and to what truly matters.

Many early readers told me they felt a sense of calm after finishing *Kill the Chameleon*. That made me smile. A calm mind is indeed a gift – it's the ground from which clarity and wise decisions grow.

But sometimes calm needs a spark to turn awareness into action. Your nature isn't a mistake; it's here to bring value to the world, whether that's to a neighbour, client, or colleague.

So take your ideas and put them into practice. Experiment. Apply them. See what happens.

If you'd like to share what unfolds, I'd genuinely love to hear from you. You can send me your reflections, insights, and stories through **killthechameleon.com.au**. While you're there, you can also join our mailing list to be among the first to know when new courses, books, or resources are released – all designed to help you build a business (and a life) that truly fits *you*.

Wishing you a life and business of clarity and authenticity.

Matt Linnert

www.ingramcontent.com/pod-product-compliance
Lightning Source LLC
Chambersburg PA
CBHW030321080526
44584CB00012B/651